ANTEBELLUM AND CIVIL WAR SAN FRANCISCO

A Western Theater for Northern & Southern Politics

Monika Trobits

THE History PRESS

Published by The History Press
Charleston, SC 29403
www.historypress.net

Copyright © 2014 by Monika Trobits
All rights reserved

Front cover, top left: William M. Gwin. *Library of Congress.*
Front cover, top middle: Lillie Hitchcock and Dr. Charles Hitchcock. *San Francisco History Center, San Francisco Public Library.*
Front cover, top right: David C. Broderick. *Library of Congress.*
Front and back covers, bottom: An 1851 panorama of San Francisco and Yerba Buena Cove looking toward the East Bay. *San Francisco Maritime NHP, A11.7881.2n.*
Back cover, top left: An 1856 Vigilance Committee mêlée. *San Francisco History Center, San Francisco Public Library.*
Back cover, top right: Metropolitan Theatre interior. *San Francisco History Center, San Francisco Public Library.*

First published 2014

Manufactured in the United States

ISBN 978.1.62619.427.4

Library of Congress Control Number: 2014953161

Notice: The information in this book is true and complete to the best of our knowledge. It is offered without guarantee on the part of the author or The History Press. The author and The History Press disclaim all liability in connection with the use of this book.

All rights reserved. No part of this book may be reproduced or transmitted in any form whatsoever without prior written permission from the publisher except in the case of brief quotations embodied in critical articles and reviews.

Contents

Introduction	5
1. A Lightning Message from the East	9
2. The Booths in San Francisco	12
3. From Alta California to the State of California	18
4. San Francisco Dramas	27
5. The Thirty-First State	40
6. Leading Players: New Englanders, New Yorkers and Southerners	48
7. Illicit Acts	61
8. The Next Act	65
9. Political Theater	70
10. San Francisco Players	80
11. The Shadow of War in San Francisco	88
12. The Curtain Falls	102
13. Remaining Players	109
Appendix. Sites and Streets Related to the Antebellum and Civil War Eras in San Francisco	121
Notes	125
Bibliography	133
Index	139
About the Author	143

Introduction

From the era of the British colonies to the emergence of the American states, the eastern seaboard had been both slave and free. As the country grew westward, that trend continued but became increasingly more and more complicated. The Louisiana Purchase in 1803 doubled the size of the country and created new debates over the westward expansion of slavery. As Northerners and Southerners began slowly moving into the vast Louisiana Territory, merging with the longtime French, Spanish and tribal residents, it would take congressional acts and compromises to maintain the increasingly shaky equilibrium. Forty-five years later, American acquisition of Mexican Alta California and the simultaneous discovery of gold created an unprecedented rush to the West, raising new questions about the expansion of slavery. The current state of California would be carved out of that acquisition amid congressional arguments both in favor of and against extending slavery to the West.

By the mid-nineteenth century, Southern interests in Congress, which represented slaveholding aristocrats, appeared to be paralleling the British Parliament of the eighteenth century. Parliament had imposed controls and restrictions on its thirteen colonies in North America, the very same colonies that would emerge as the East Coast states of the North and the South. But did Congress want to risk driving Americans to rebellion, as had happened in 1776, resulting in a long, drawn-out war? A civil war would be even worse than a revolution. Americans would be fighting one another during emotionally charged, passion-filled, bloody battles that

Introduction

would ravage the landscape and its residents. Many Americans could see the similarities between the United States of the 1850s and the British colonies in the 1770s. Some could see only the economics of the increasingly worn-out fields in the East as decades of plantation-style farming took its toll. To them, the need to continue extending slavery farther and farther west was obvious and justified. A good number, however, believed that each individual state should decide the question for itself. While Congress debated back and forth, those already in California in 1849 took matters into their own hands and did just that.

More than two thousand miles separated California from the political, social and economic dynamics of the states that comprised the North and the South. It would attract those dynamics to the West as thousands of highly motivated individuals steadily poured into San Francisco from regions east of the Mississippi River, destined for the nearby gold fields. The antebellum era in the eastern states coincided with the gold rush era in California, and the social order that developed out of this gold rush migration in many ways represented a microcosm of the United States in the 1850s. These American gold seekers brought with them their respective politics and their attitudes reflecting the economic and social realities of either the industrial, money-oriented North or the social status consciousness and chivalry of the agricultural South. Their migration would introduce both the New York– and Southern-style of politics to San Francisco beginning in 1849. This divergence would play out in interesting ways over the coming decade, i.e., through feuds, duels and the loss and gain of political control. These American newcomers would join the very diverse collection of individuals already in California who had arrived the prior year, during previous decades or over the course of many centuries.

San Francisco became the new El Dorado. What had been a small town of fewer than one thousand residents in 1848 would burst into a booming city of thirty thousand within two years; an instant city, it was called. While a significant number of its transient residents were foreigners from various continents, the Americans from the Atlantic states would dominate. If East Coasters thought they had moved away from the heated slavery question by going west, they were wrong, as it followed them to the shores of the Pacific. The rush for California's mineral riches of gold and, later, silver during the antebellum period would force some Argonauts to choose between the wealth of the West and loyalty to the South. It also forced Congress and the nation to confront the future of the South's peculiar institution and its

Introduction

application in the West. These issues pushed the United States toward its second American revolution, the Civil War.

The West would prove to be more than a distant relative to the squabbling siblings of the North and the South. Following the war, it would be where the flagging, puritanical American work ethic of the East would be reborn as the energized, entrepreneurial California dream of the West. San Francisco would become the Queen City of America's West, and California would emerge as the Empire State of the Pacific.

One important point that readers should bear in mind is with respect to political parties as they are discussed in this book. In both platform and philosophy, the Democrats and Republicans of the mid-nineteenth century were dramatically different from the parties bearing the same names in the modern era.

The idea for this book came about because of my continued interest in San Francisco's early years, my longtime love of the theater and my wanting to know more about the impact of the Civil War in the West. What brought it all together for me was my reading about the Booth acting family and how antebellum issues affected them. In many respects, the Booths are the bookends for the story in this book.

In the interest of the past meeting with the present, I have sought to connect San Francisco's antebellum and Civil War days with present-day life in the city by highlighting the remnants from those decisive, unsettling decades of the mid-nineteenth century. I do much the same through a walking tour that I have developed in conjunction with this book. More information on that tour may be found on my website: www.sanfranciscojourneys.com.

Monika Trobits
San Francisco, California
October 2014

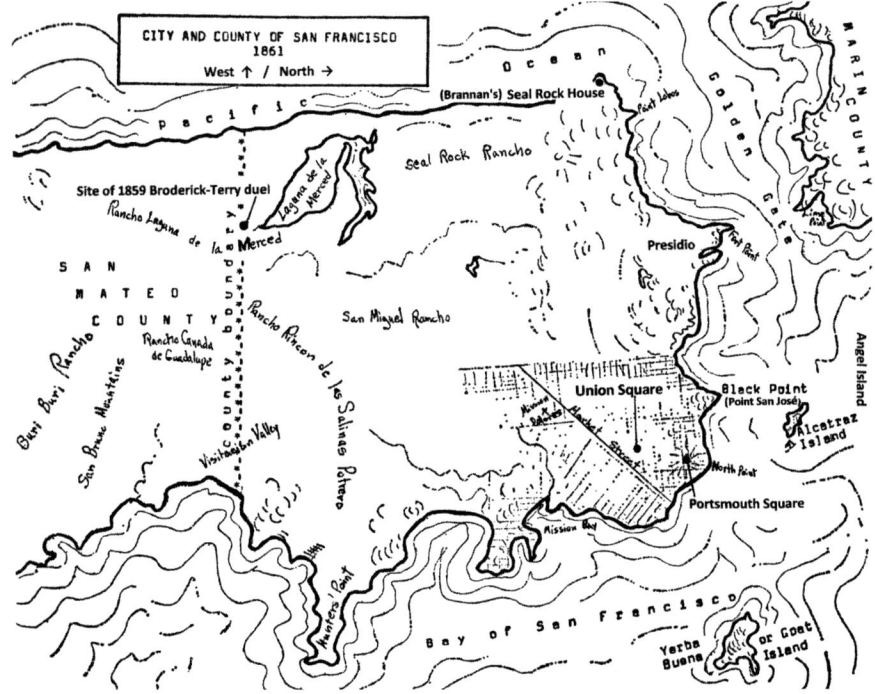

An 1861 map of San Francisco annotated by the author. *Courtesy Rather Press Collection, Sanoian Special Collections Library, California State University, Fresno.*

Chapter 1

A Lightning Message from the East

The telegram arrived in San Francisco at 10:00 a.m.[1] It was an official bulletin, the first of several, and the operator on duty immediately posted it in the front window for all to read. The news it conveyed was astounding, almost unbelievable, and had rapidly traveled along wires that stretched from the nation's capital to the western edge of the continent. Twenty-year-old Charles de Young listened to the taps of the telegraph's vigorous rhythmic dance while he examined the already posted telegrams. He was looking for items to fill the pages of his fledgling afternoon paper, the *Daily Dramatic Chronicle*. As a co-founder of the three-month-old *Chronicle*, it was his practice to stop by the telegraph office on his way to his own nearby office. The telegraphic clicking of the incoming message continued and de Young, who knew Morse code, could scarcely believe his ears. The telegram announced that the president had been shot and, nine hours later, had died. The message went on to say that the shooting had taken place in a theater in Washington, D.C. Subsequent dispatches would reveal that the assassination had occurred the night before at Ford's Theatre, during the third act of a popular play. Pushing his way through the growing crowd, Charles de Young rushed over to his Clay Street office a few blocks away, armed with the incredible news of Saturday, April 15, 1865.

Charles and Gustavus de Young had characterized their newspaper as "The Abstract and Brief Chronicle of the Times: Local, Critical, Musical and Theatrical." That mission statement was noted on the front page of every edition. Unbeknownst to them, their pro-Union *Chronicle* was at the turning point of becoming much more, as on that mid-April day, it would be the first paper in San Francisco to print the dispatches about President Lincoln's assassination. By the time those dispatches arrived, morning editions of the *Daily Alta California* and the *Morning Call* had already been published and distributed; their staffs had left for the day. The de Youngs realized they had been gifted with an extraordinary scoop and hurried to get the pages of their tabloid-style paper printed and into the hands of their readers. However, as important as the news was, it would be noted on page two. As usual, the front page was reserved for the paid listing of a playbill for the day's featured theatrical performance. On opposite margins would be listings of related revenue-producing advertising. Advertising paid the bills and would not be moved off the front page, not even for a presidential assassination.

San Francisco's booming and growing theater business encouraged the founding of the *Daily Dramatic Chronicle* on January 16, 1865. Within three months, its circulation had already grown to four thousand[2] in the city that boasted more than sixty thousand residents. The Lincoln assassination articles would rapidly boost circulation to five thousand. The de Youngs had established their theatrical daily in a city in which newspapers were as essential to everyday life as were its many saloons and theaters. On that April 15 day, their free theater daily would be distributed throughout the city in its saloons, gambling houses and restaurants; its boardinghouses and hotels; and, as the afternoon turned into evening, within its theaters. Subsequent telegraphed bulletins would necessitate extra editions.

The *Daily Dramatic Chronicle*'s Monday edition[3] included a woodcut image of the alleged assassin himself: the strikingly handsome, popular and melodramatic actor John Wilkes Booth, who had immediately fled Ford's Theatre and the city of Washington following his shooting of Lincoln. A known Southern sympathizer, Booth would be aggressively

Masthead from the April 14, 1865 edition of the *Daily Dramatic Chronicle. Courtesy San Francisco Public Library.*

pursued by Federal troops as he escaped the nation's capital, hurriedly riding south through Maryland and into rural northern Virginia. He would be found hiding in a tobacco barn on April 26. When he refused to surrender himself, the barn was set ablaze, and the twenty-six-year-old Booth was shot.

Chapter 2

The Booths in San Francisco

By the mid-1860s, the Booth theatrical family of Maryland was well known in San Francisco. John Wilkes's eldest brother, Junius Brutus Booth Jr., nicknamed "June," had arrived in San Francisco in 1851. He was about thirty and had traveled west with his then-mistress, Harriet Mace, a pretty, young actress from Boston. They moved into a cottage on Signal (now Telegraph) Hill and joined Tom Maguire's stock theater company. Both appeared in the production of *All That Glitters Is Not Gold* at Maguire's new Jenny Lind Theatre that October. The following spring, June and Harriet traveled to Baltimore for a visit with the Booth family. A few months later, they were on their way back to San Francisco, accompanied by June's father, well-known actor Junius Brutus Booth Sr., and his younger brother Edwin, then nineteen. Edwin was a fledgling actor whose main job was to keep an eye on his aging, hard-drinking and sometimes mentally unstable father. June had encouraged them both to join him and Harriet in San Francisco, telling them it was a growing city of approximately fifty thousand residents, many of whom welcomed high-quality theatrical entertainment. He spoke of the potential for lucrative earnings, often paid in pure gold. June told his father that the whole world was heading to San Francisco, and so should he. Curious about the opportunities in San Francisco and in desperate need of money, Junius Sr. considered June's words and saw the possibilities of profitable adventures in the West.

They set out on the long and arduous westward journey, finally sailing through the Golden Gate on the morning of July 28, 1852, on the *California*.

A Western Theater for Northern & Southern Politics

The four survived the thirty-seven-day journey that had begun with sailing southward from New York, then crossing the tropical jungles and swamps of the Panamanian Isthmus and continuing through northern Pacific waters to San Francisco. Upon their arrival at the "Long Wharf" (aka the Commercial Street Wharf), the Booths were greeted with a brass band and enthusiastically welcomed by a large gathering of San Francisco residents. Already, there was growing anticipation of the upcoming theatrical performances by the Booths, but in particular by Junius Sr., the great tragedian actor of his day. In its July 30, 1852 edition, the *Daily Alta California* noted: "The arrival of the tragedian will arouse and revive drooping theatricals in the state. The name is sufficient in itself; it needs no commentary."

All the Booths had roles in the various plays that were subsequently performed during the first half of August. These included *The Iron Chest*, *Hamlet*, *Macbeth* and *Richard III*. These performances took place at the city's largest and costliest building to date, the (third) Jenny Lind Theatre across from Portsmouth Square, the heart of the city at the time. It was to the Booths' advantage that June was manager of the two-thousand-seat Jenny Lind. He had orchestrated their two-week engagement there, and it was the success that June had foreseen, as performance after performance saw every seat in the house filled. Standing room–only patrons would pack every available space right up to the exit doors. Its owner and local theater entrepreneur, Tom Maguire, had provided the brass band at the Long Wharf. Maguire, an astute businessman, knew a good deal when he saw one, and in the summer of 1852, he saw two: the profitable two-week engagement of the Booth family players at his theater and the subsequent sale of the theater building itself, then less than a year old, to the city. The sale was arranged by Maguire's politically connected good friend and boarder David Broderick. The theater was purchased by the city for $200,000 and was shortly thereafter converted into San Francisco's city hall.

Following well-received performances in San Francisco but greeted with only a lukewarm reception in Sacramento along with heavy rains, Junius Sr. returned to the city for farewell performances at the Adelphi Theater, appearing in *A New Way to Pay Old Debts*, among other plays. On October 1, 1852, he sailed out of San Francisco on the *Independence* to return to the family homestead in Maryland. Junius Sr.'s eastbound trip included a trek across Nicaragua to the Atlantic coast. Along the way, he was robbed of all his California earnings, leaving him penniless and stranded. A fellow traveler, a rich and admiring Texan named Reid, recognized Booth and felt sorry for him. Reid purchased his

San Francisco's city hall (the former Jenny Lind Theatre) on Kearny Street across from Portsmouth Square, circa 1850s. In 1854, this block of Kearny became the city's first paved street. *Courtesy Library of Congress.*

passage on the steamer *Daniel Webster*, sailing to New Orleans. Once there, Booth managed to secure an engagement at that city's ornate St. Charles Theatre, earning $1,000 for six performances. That was more than enough for him to continue with his travels home to Maryland. A personal tragedy then struck the tragedian. Junius Sr. unexpectedly died of dysentery while traveling on a Mississippi steamboat bound for Cincinnati. Suffering from a bad cold, the unsupervised Booth indulged in alcohol during his river journey. He then unwisely chose to freely drink from the cloudy waters of the Mississippi. Poor overall health and a lack of proper medical attention hastened his death at age fifty-six. A telegram was dispatched from Louisville addressed to Booth's wife, Mary Ann, in Maryland. It was sent by the steamboat's captain and advised that Mr. Booth was gravely ill. Mrs. Booth met the boat in Cincinnati and was shocked to discover that Junius was, in fact, dead. Stunned at the news of her husband's death, Mrs. Booth had no choice but to accompany his body back to Baltimore, where four of her younger children,[4] including her favorite son, John Wilkes, then fourteen, awaited.

A Western Theater for Northern & Southern Politics

June, Harriet and Edwin had stayed on in San Francisco. A letter arrived in December from Mary Ann Booth with the surprising news of Junius's death and advising them to remain in California. They all did so, continuing to pursue various local theatrical opportunities. June acted here and there but was far more successful as a theater manager. During his years in San Francisco, he managed the Metropolitan, the San Francisco and the Union Theatres, in addition to the Jenny Lind. These theaters often featured Edwin Booth in plays such as *Box and Cox*, a minstrel show that required blackface; *Trip to California*; *Crossing the Isthmus*; and *The American Fireman*. Edwin would also appear in other local theaters, including the American and Maguire's Opera House. Under June's tutelage, Edwin concentrated on further developing and refining his acting skills through his performances in San Francisco.

This interior view of the Metropolitan Theatre depicts Edwin Booth on stage in a supporting role as Sir Thomas Clifford during an 1854 performance of *The Hunchback*. *Courtesy San Francisco History Center, San Francisco Public Library.*

When the local San Francisco economy stagnated, Edwin embarked on a theatrical tour of Australia with British actress Laura Keene. Keene had successfully performed on both American coasts and would go on to manage theaters in San Francisco and New York. The two began the tour as close collaborators and ended it barely speaking to each other. Keene was outraged by Edwin's irresponsible behavior during the tour, particularly his excessive drinking. Edwin, meanwhile, grew tired of Keene's impatience and temper tantrums. All that combined with a downturn in the Australian economy hurt ticket sales and cut into the profits Keene hoped to realize. Edwin's reputation was somewhat redeemed by his subsequent performances in Samoa, Tahiti and the Sandwich (Hawaiian) Islands in 1855 during stops made on his way back to San Francisco.

While Edwin was traveling in the South Seas, June had again visited his family in Maryland, including his now-widowed mother. He became concerned about her leniency with his brother John, whom he found to be undisciplined, headstrong and wanting nothing but his late father's fame. June particularly noted that John's friends were the sons of prominent slaveholding Southern families. Upon returning to San Francisco, June shared his observations with Edwin. Edwin listened quietly and thoughtfully, knowing that Maryland was a divided state.

In September 1856, after four years in San Francisco, Edwin sailed out through the Golden Gate on the *Golden Age*. While still locally popular, he had determined that success in the West was not enough for an actor with his potential. He needed to emulate his late father and theatrically tour the eastern half of the country as well, bringing his own merit to his famous surname and broadening his individual reputation in front of new audiences. Booth traveled east via Panama, enjoying comfortable and protected travel across its isthmus in a railway car. Arduous treks across the isthmus had ended with the completion of the Panama Railroad. Now, the train completed the forty-seven-mile route in three hours at a fare of twenty-five dollars in gold for a one-way ticket. The cost was not a burden for Edwin, whose coffer was filled with his share of the proceeds for his San Francisco performances, particularly his final run as King Lear at the Metropolitan Theatre. Thunderous applause during the play could be heard by nearby residents, including William Tecumseh Sherman. Sherman was then managing the local branch of the Bank of Lucas, Turner and Co. across the street[5] and lived on its upper level.

The sudden death of the celebrated Shakespearean actor Junius Brutus Booth Sr. not only distressed his family financially but also activated what would become a simmering rivalry between his sons June and Edwin, who had taken their turns traveling with their father throughout the East's theatrical circuit, and John Wilkes, who had remained behind in Maryland with their mother and had never even seen his father perform on the stage. John grew handsome, but his lack of discipline and unwillingness to be directed would curtail his career; his impulsive and pretentious acting style would generate mixed reviews. Had he come to San Francisco, John would have likely benefitted from June's guidance and training, but he never did. Instead, it was Edwin who was destined to be the rising star of the family. It was he who had truly inherited his father's talent, which Edwin would cultivate into a much less dramatic and much more natural style. Through their mother, John Wilkes would eventually be gifted with their father's superb collection of theatrical costumes; she denied them to a disappointed Edwin. Prior to Junius Sr.'s departure from San Francisco, he had gifted June, his eldest son, with the jeweled diadem he wore while portraying Richard III. Junius told June and Edwin that he would no longer need the crown, as he planned to retire from the stage.

During the next ten years, the brothers endured constant comparisons regularly made between one another and with their late father. June and his family remained in San Francisco, where he continued acting and managing theaters. Edwin performed mainly in the North. John Wilkes performed in both Northern and Southern cities, returning again and again to Richmond, Virginia, where he was particularly well received. Edwin was determined to keep John out of New York City, as it had become the capital city of the American theater and offered a diversity of roles, substantial monetary rewards and recognition from larger and more sophisticated audiences. He viewed New York as his own domain and preferred that his younger brother performed elsewhere, such as in Southern cities. John, for his part, was comfortable in the South and sympathetic to Southern politics and ideology. He was not alone in his predispositions.

Chapter 3

From Alta California to the State of California

In the late summer of 1849, several dozen California delegates gathered for an important convention in the *Pueblo de Monterey*. The town, consisting of about 1,500 residents, had from 1776 to the mid-1840s been the capital of Alta (upper) California for the Spanish Empire and then for the Republic of Mexico. Spanish/Mexican Alta California included today's states of California, Nevada and Utah, as well as portions of Arizona, Colorado, New Mexico and Wyoming. This entire landmass, approximately 525,000 square miles, had been claimed by Spain as part of its empire as early as the sixteenth century but was lost to Mexico by 1821. In 1846, the United States instigated a war with Mexico after more diplomatic attempts to acquire Alta California had failed. As part of that conquest, the twenty-eight-star American flag was first raised in the West over Monterey's customhouse on July 7, 1846, by Commodore John Drake Sloat. Two days later, 120 miles to the north, another U.S. flag would be raised by Captain John Montgomery of the USS *Portsmouth* in the middle of the Mexican Plaza, which was the heart of *El Paraje de Yerba Buena* (The Place of the Good Herb). Yerba Buena would be renamed San Francisco in 1847. The raising of these flags occurred without protest and officially established American authority in Mexican Alta California in the early days of the war. The landmass was destined to become the westernmost possession of the United States by early 1848. The Treaty of Guadalupe Hidalgo, which officially ended the war with Mexico, was signed in Mexico City on February 2, 1848, and the land became officially known as the Mexican Cession. The signing of the treaty took place just nine days after a very significant discovery of gold along the banks of the *Rio de los Americanos* (the American River) just about 150 miles northeast of San Francisco. This golden news eventually made its way to Northerners and Southerners in the East, luring them to a place few had ever heard of but that beckoned with potentially exciting adventures and instant wealth, the likes of which most had never before experienced.

The first of three reports of the gold discovery arrived in Washington in August 1848 in the hands of Christopher "Kit" Carson, a frontiersman, scout and courier. Carson's military superiors sent him east with letters telling of the discovery along with a copy of the *California Star* newspaper. The news arrived in Washington for a second time in September in the form of a letter written by Thomas Larkin, U.S. consul in Mexican Alta California since 1843 and President James K. Polk's emissary. Larkin's letter, which carried more weight, was addressed to Secretary of State James Buchanan and was brought to the White House by naval officer Edward Beale. Beale also brought along a few gold nuggets to confirm the discovery. Polk was initially skeptical of both reports, however, and held off on making any formal announcements about the discovery. Colonel Richard B. Mason, Alta California's military governor, sent the official report of the gold discovery directly to the attention of the president. It arrived in November and was accompanied by 230 ounces of gold dust stuffed into a metal tea caddy, which was subsequently put on display at the War Department. President Polk was finally convinced that the gold discovery was real. So were many others after reading copies of Mason's report.

During his State of the Union speech to Congress and the nation in December 1848, Polk formally announced that an "abundance of gold" had been discovered in the land recently acquired from Mexico, noting that it would more than recompense for the cost of the recent war. Congress, however, had adjourned in the spring of 1848 without formally establishing Alta California's status. This was due to its inability to come to terms with the potential application of slavery in the newly acquired western lands. It did, however, decide that federal tax codes would apply to those lands. In San Francisco, this led to protests that Congress was taxing without representation and without designation for a local government, i.e., the burden of government without any of its benefits. Echoes of King George III indeed!

Alta California would remain an American possession and continue to be governed by military authorities who ruled by right of conquest. A new military governor, Brigadier General Bennet Riley, arrived in Alta California on June 3, 1849. He concluded that a military system as a governing force was inadequate during peacetime, especially in light of the new rush to San Francisco and the imposition of federal taxation. Some kind of government, either territorial or state, would need to be organized and a convention held to accomplish that. Riley issued a proclamation for holding a constitutional forum in Monterey to determine the best form of government for Alta California. He then called for an area-wide election of delegates to take place on August 1 for the purpose of drawing up a formal constitution that would either lead to statehood or organize a territorial government.

President Zachary Taylor sent Representative Thomas Butler King to San Francisco in mid-1849 to survey the political particulars and to discretely encourage a movement for statehood. King was a Massachusetts native who had been educated in Pennsylvania as a lawyer. After moving to Georgia, he married into a slave-owning family and inherited a coastal plantation. King, however, preferred politics, and after serving in the Georgia legislature, he was elected to the U.S. House of Representatives. In Washington, he allied with the Whig Party and was appointed as Taylor's envoy to Alta California. Upon arrival, King found that the process to officially determine Alta California's status was already underway. To facilitate travel to the constitutional convention, King used his federally granted authority to engage a steamship to pick up convention delegates from southern Alta California ports and transport them up to Monterey.

King saw opportunities for himself in the West and in mid-June organized a rally for statehood in San Francisco's old Mexican Plaza, by then known as Portsmouth Square. States had senators, and King aimed to be one representing California. A large poster depicting an American eagle with a banner in its beak declaring "THE PEOPLE MUST RULE!" was displayed in the square. On the flagpole in front of the customhouse flew the thirty-star U.S. flag, fluttering in the afternoon winds. The scene provided a backdrop for the three speakers: William M. Gwin, a well-educated Southerner, physician, lawyer and Mississippi plantation owner; Peter Burnett, a Tennessee-born lawyer who grew up in Missouri; and King himself, whose speech was rather self-serving. Gwin and King then embarked on separate speaking tours to generate interest in the convention and the selection of delegates.

On September 1, 1849, forty-eight elected delegates representing ten districts assembled in Colton Hall, a meetinghouse in Monterey, for the constitutional convention. U.S. consul Larkin welcomed the very diverse group. A New Englander, Larkin was himself a delegate, one of six representing Monterey. The delegation represented the diversity of

A Western Theater for Northern & Southern Politics

Alta California. Thirty-seven of the delegates were originally from the East—twenty-two from Northern states and fifteen from Southern states. Seven were native Mexican *Californios*. Also present were six foreign-born delegates. Fourteen of the delegates were lawyers, eleven were ranchmen and seven were merchants. Twenty-seven were less than thirty-five years old, while three were over fifty. The largest number of delegates came from New York. With only one small local hotel, the delegates lodged with residents in private homes and in nearby army barracks or simply camped under the trees during the six-week convention. Larkin and his wife welcomed several delegates into their home, including William Gwin. The activities surrounding the 1849 constitutional convention event in Monterey would serve to mark the twilight of the Spanish/Mexican capital's dominance in California and the old way of life it represented. The future was in San Francisco.

A total of eight delegates represented the emerging city of San Francisco at the convention. These included the aforementioned Gwin. Also present were Joseph Hobson, a merchant, and William Steuart, a lawyer, both from the border state of Maryland. Five Northerners were also among the San Francisco delegates. Among them were two New Yorkers: Edward Gilbert, senior editor of the *Daily Alta California*, who reported on the convention's proceedings, and Alfred J. Ellis, a popular and respected merchant who

Completed in March 1849, Colton Hall in Monterey was the site of the California Constitutional Convention later that year. *Courtesy of the author.*

Thomas Larkin's 1835 Monterey home, where he hosted convention delegates. *Courtesy of the author.*

ran a saloon and boardinghouse. Gilbert had previously written a series of editorials that encouraged Riley to organize the convention. Ellis would later serve on two San Francisco Vigilance Committees during the 1850s. Other San Francisco delegates were Myron Norton (Vermont), a lawyer who was prominent in the early days of the city but would move to Los Angeles in 1852; Rodman Price (New Jersey), a naval officer during the Mexican-American War and a prefect and *alcalde* (mayor/sheriff/judge) in 1846 for Monterey; and Francis J. Lippitt (Rhode Island), also a war veteran and a future colonel for the Union army.

The convention was open to the public, and among its attendees were the famed western explorer John C. Frémont and his eloquent wife, Jessie Benton Frémont, both abolitionists. Like the Larkins, the Frémonts also welcomed delegates as guests into their Monterey home, particularly the antislavery delegates. Also received were convention attendees Lieutenant William Sherman, an observer on behalf of General Persifor Smith, commander of the Pacific Division, and Bayard Taylor, a reporter for the *New York Tribune*.

An oil portrait of George Washington hung on Colton Hall's east wall, silently observing the delegation. Refreshing late summer breezes from nearby Monterey Bay wafted in when the balcony doors were opened in the afternoons. Reflecting California's bilingual environment, the proceedings took place in both English and Spanish. The state constitutions for Iowa and New York were used as guides. Deliberations continued for six weeks, with a myriad of issues considered for inclusion into the constitution. These included compromises regarding taxation, a great concern among the delegates from the southern districts and their constituents. The eastern border for the intended state of California was initially suggested at 116 degrees longitude following debates about making all of Alta California a single state, albeit a very large free state, which would eliminate the issue of extending slavery to the West. Since it was also likely to delay statehood altogether, it was instead agreed that the new state's eastern border would be the Sierra Nevada mountain range and that the remaining portions of the Alta California landmass would be divided into territories. Delegates decided to continue a provision of Mexican law that allowed women to retain sole ownership of any property they brought into a marriage. This was done to encourage well-off women to come to California, where 92 percent of the population was male. Divorce and lotteries were prohibited.

Keenly aware of rising tensions in the eastern states, the delegates, after much discussion, opted to outlaw slavery and indentured servitude. Doing so continued the ban instituted in 1829 by Mexico for Mexican Alta California. The decision was unanimous based on the widely held opinion that California's weather and soil were, for the most part, not suitable for extensive agricultural development. Hotly debated (for two entire days) was the issue of banning free blacks, emancipated blacks or contracted black laborers from entering California and working in its mines. While

Colton Hall's second-floor interior, ready for the arrival of the 1849 Constitutional Convention delegates. *Courtesy of the author.*

this would be voted down, the delegates then "voted to disenfranchise 'Indians, Africans and the descendants of Africans,'"[6] thus denying them citizenship and the ability to own land in the West. The delegates signed the constitution in mid-October and designated *Pueblo de los San José* as the new capital. Delegate Steuart drafted the "Address to the People," which stated the case for the approval of the new constitution. The secretary of state for the convention, Henry W. Halleck (New York), a delegate representing Monterey, was dispatched to San Francisco posthaste with directions for the printing of the pending constitution. Copies were produced in pamphlet form for distribution. The printing, which would be done at the offices of the *Daily Alta California*, included six thousand copies printed in English and two thousand in Spanish. Most of the copies printed in English went to the northern districts of Alta California; most of those printed in Spanish were sent down to the southern districts. William Gwin set off to actively campaign area-wide for the passage of the new constitution and to ingratiate himself with aspiring candidates for the state legislature who would potentially support him for senator. The vote was held on November 13, 1849, and turnout was light, possibly complicated by cold, rainy weather; rising water; and muddy roads in the northern districts. Only 15 percent of eligible voters actually voted; 12,061 were in favor of the new constitution, 811 against. In the San Francisco district, 2,051 voted in favor, while 5 were against. Most potential voters were too busy trying to get rich in the gold fields to concern themselves with a newly drawn-up constitution.

Suffering from a severe case of dysentery that waylaid him for three months, Thomas Butler King missed the convention's proceedings but was pleased with its outcome and the subsequent approval of the new constitution. He was regarded by many, including Sherman, as the government candidate for the U.S. Senate representing the potential new state of California in Congress. King could certainly see himself in that role and, in anticipation, had resigned his congressional seat in a letter sent to the governor of Georgia.

Prior to adjourning the convention, and in anticipation of statehood, delegates set up a pseudo-state government that would operate in the interim. Governor Reilly then surrendered his role as administrator of civil affairs in California, and Henry Halleck was relieved of his duties as military secretary. Technically speaking, all of the convention procedures were illegal, as were the elections of Peter Burnett as civilian governor, a state legislature and the subsequent legislative election of senators

A Western Theater for Northern & Southern Politics

California senator and slaveholder William M. Gwin. *Courtesy Library of Congress.*

and representatives for if/when California became a state. At the first state legislative session in San José, on December 15, leading senatorial candidates Gwin and Frémont and their rivals, including King and Halleck, plied the state legislators with free drinks in the hopes of getting their respective votes, leading to this first session to be referred to as the "legislature of a thousand drinks." After many ballots (and presumably, many drinks), the winning candidates were John C. Frémont, the popular western explorer, and William M. Gwin, the Mississippi slaveholder. It then had to be determined who would serve which term. Frémont drew the short straw and the shorter term, which would end in March 1851. Gwin would serve the full six-year term. Also elected were two representatives to the House of Representatives: Edward Gilbert and George W. Wright. Wright (Massachusetts) had mining and banking interests in San Francisco.

Gwin was not pleased with the outcome, as he viewed Frémont as a hypocrite who had no qualms about killing tribal Indians and *Californios* but was sentimental about slaves, who, having monetary value, were in Gwin's view treated far better in the long run.

King's ambitions for a Senate seat had been quashed. He returned to San Francisco, co-founding a law office there. Certain that statehood was just around the corner, King elected to position himself in San Francisco and to remain in the West at least for the immediate future.

On New Year's Day 1850, the prospective congressional delegation sailed out of San Francisco on the *Oregon* en route to Washington carrying copies of the new California constitution. Also on board were Jessie Frémont, William Sherman and Thomas Butler King. Upon arrival, copies were distributed to the high-ranking members of all three branches of the federal government. The delegation then found itself on the front lines of the ongoing congressional battle over slavery, to which was added the debate regarding the potential admission of California as the thirty-first state. Objections were raised in Congress regarding the irregularity of the framing of the potential new state's constitution. Doing so had allowed California to self-determine the issue of slavery. Also questioned was the size of the potential state itself and the fact that many of California's residents in 1850, particularly in its southern districts, were not citizens of the United States but rather Mexican *Californios*.

Chapter 4

San Francisco Dramas

Political differences that would come to divide the Booth brothers had already begun to divide the eastern half of the country. Alta California would not escape these tensions when thousands of highly motivated men from both the North and South poured into San Francisco beginning in 1849. The social order that developed out of this gold rush migration resulted in California becoming the most representative state of the United States during the 1850s.

News traveled by sea in the old days, and for much of 1848, accounts about the discovery of gold had been spread by ships that occasionally visited the isolated, foggy port of San Francisco. The very first reports about the gold discovery mainly traveled west and south to Pacific ports in Asia, South America and Australia, attracting the first waves of gold seekers and marking the beginning of San Francisco's diversity. President Polk's announcement in late 1848 sparked the American rush of Northerners and Southerners. It inspired westward treks across the continent through tribal lands and western territories that featured topography that most of those travelers had never before seen. Those who could afford the costly passage went by sea, traveling the traditional route around the Horn, sailing on two oceans for an expedition that would often take more than six months and covered as much as eighteen thousand nautical miles. Still other adventurers, like the Booths, combined the land and sea methods, which included trekking across the Isthmus of Panama in poled boats and on pack mules and risking exposure to jungle (yellow) fever or cholera, injury from local bandits or death from both. Arriving ships would sail through the magnificent portal to San Francisco Bay, known as the Golden Gate Straits. This portal had been aptly named in 1847 by explorer and future U.S. senator John C. Frémont, ninety years before the bridge spanning the channel would take on the same name.[7] Sentries, manning the lookout station on the crest of Signal (later Telegraph) Hill, would signal the type of incoming vessel using the black arms of their semaphore. A total of 777 vessels sailed through the Golden Gate in 1849; fewer than a half dozen had come through just two years earlier.

By 1849, the former hamlet of Yerba Buena with just about eight hundred[8] residents had become the booming American city of San Francisco; by 1850, it would accommodate approximately thirty thousand transient residents. Portsmouth Square was the hub of the new city. The name of the nearby and oldest street, *La Calle de la Fundación* (The Street of the Founding), was changed to Dupont Street (and, later, to Grant Avenue). Numerous ships, cargo and passenger, regularly sailed into Yerba Buena Cove, carrying more and more new residents for the growing city and the nearby gold fields. As the months passed, a forest of ships' masts crowded the cove.

Upon arrival, travelers would find that San Francisco was both a frontier town and a tent city. Most of these tents were made using the canvas from the sails of the hundreds of ships that were left abandoned on the tidal flats of the cove. The streets were ankle-deep in sand during the dry months and in mud during the rainy season. The surrounding treeless hills were covered in sand, which was often blown about by the afternoon winds. The area immediately around Portsmouth Square contained fewer than two hundred permanent structures (generally adobe and wood prior to 1851, mainly brick thereafter[9]) during those early days. At the time, the shoreline was at present-day Montgomery Street (originally Water Street), one block east of Portsmouth Square and a pathway up the hillside of Signal Hill.

In July 1849, the *Niantic* sailed into Yerba Buena Cove carrying 246 passengers, including 1 slave. Its crew followed most of the passengers to the gold fields. Left docked at the Clay Street Wharf, the *Niantic* was sold and was among the first ships to be turned into a store ship, then office space and, by 1852, a very fine hotel. Its enterprising owner hung out a sign that read:

Rest for the Weary
and
Storage for Trunks[10]

A Western Theater for Northern & Southern Politics

San Francisco's first post office (pictured here circa 1850) opened in November 1848 at Pike (Waverly Place) and Clay Streets. Long lines and lost mail were common. *Courtesy Library of Congress.*

By 1850, more than six hundred abandoned ships—passenger and cargo—were sitting in the cove with no crews to sail them back out. Those docked on the front lines of the waterfront were literally stuck in place, and many served as saloons and much-needed hotels and sailors' boardinghouses. Ships' captains often found themselves in a new role: as innkeepers renting out the berths on their vessels. Planks would often be torn off the abandoned ships and used for building or as much-needed firewood. But these ships would need to be moved out, as local officials had decided in 1849 to begin filling in the crescent-shaped cove that extended south to Folsom Street and north to Broadway. Sand from the surrounding dunes and downtown hills was used for much of the fill, but many of the abandoned ships were sunk in place, contributing to the landfill. Everything and anything was thrown into the cove to help fill it, leading to interesting modern-day discoveries. Work continued on through 1855, eventually pushing the city's eastern shoreline out to East Street (renamed the Embarcadero in 1909).

The city's population was almost exclusively male and generally youthful (mid-teens to early forties). By the time San Francisco was incorporated as a city in April 1850, it was well on its way to becoming a multicultural city, with about half its new residents hailing from the East Coast states

A forest of ships' masts can be seen in this 1851 panorama of Yerba Buena Cove taken from Portsmouth Square. *Courtesy San Francisco Maritime NHP, A11.7881.2n.*

and the other half from foreign shores. Both groups joined the established Mexicans and Spaniards, who had been living in the area for almost one hundred years, and the members of the Ohlone tribe, which had been there for many thousands. The mix of the city's population was reflected in the English-language and foreign-language newspapers published daily, more than a dozen by 1854.

San Francisco's reputation for being one of America's top dining destinations actually began in the 1850s, as the predominantly male population of the time regularly dined out. After all, they did not come west to cook but rather to find gold, and those who did had the means to regularly pay for top-quality meals. The cooks were among those who followed the miners, and they arrived early on, bringing with them the cuisines of the North, the South and nations beyond. One who became well known in the city was Mary Ellen Pleasant, who arrived in San Francisco in 1852. Her background was a bit of a mystery, but her extraordinary cooking skills were not. According to one account, she "sold her services at five hundred dollars a month."[11] Cooking, she informed the bidders, was her forte, quickly adding that washing was not, and that included dishwashing, which she would not do. Mrs. Pleasant cooked mainly in private households and private men's clubs before moving on to other endeavors. She was joined by skilled cooks from around the

world who produced the variety of ethnic and regional food and drink demanded by their clientele.

Canvas tent restaurants would be stocked with wild game from the area's forests, seafood from San Francisco Bay and the Pacific Ocean and beef from local ranches, many dating from the era of the *Californios*. A few of those restaurants remain in business. Tadich Grill, which started in 1849 as a small café called the Coffee Stand on the Long Wharf, still operates on California Street.[12] The Old Clam House has been housed in the same building on Bayshore Boulevard since it began in 1861. It was known as the Oakdale Bar and Clam House in its Civil War–era days. The original Cliff House was founded in 1863 and continues operating, albeit in its recently renovated 1909 building.

Three drinking establishments have survived as well. The Old Ship Saloon began in 1851 as the Old Ship Ale House in the hull of the *Arkansas*, which sailed into Yerba Buena Cove in 1849, beaching at what is now Pacific Avenue and Battery Street. Its owner cut a doorway into its hull and posted a sign reading:

> Gud, bad and indif'rent spirits sold here!
> At 25 cents each.

Landfill locked the ship in place. In 1859, the aboveground portion of the *Arkansas* was dismantled and replaced with a brick building, which became a hotel. "A barroom on the ground floor of the hotel continued the name of The Old Ship Saloon."[13]

The Elixir (1858) in the Mission District and the Saloon (1861) in North Beach also date from the era.

The first gold rush winter of 1849–50 proved to be one of the rainiest on record. Constant cold, damp weather along with driving rain and flooding took its toll on many miners. While some remained in the mining towns that had sprung up, the majority headed down to San Francisco seeking respite. Many were looking for more than just saloons, brothels and gambling houses to pass the time. They wanted real entertainment, such as theatrical productions—dramatic, comedic and Shakespearean. A select group of San Francisco's entrepreneurs would heed the call.

Theaters were among the first substantial structures built in San Francisco while most newcomers were living in tents. While some saloons, such as the Bella Union Hall, provided simple platforms for vaudeville-like presentations along the lines of black-faced minstrel shows (the first such performance would take place there in October 1849), it became apparent that actual theater venues were desired for full-fledged theatrical performances. Construction of a variety of theaters promptly began all around the Portsmouth Square area, amid the numerous saloons, gambling houses and brothels already there. Washington Hall, San Francisco's first official theater, presented its opening play on January 16, 1850. Entitled *The Wife*, it was the perfect subject for the almost entirely male audience. Performances that combined drama with the circus then began at Rowe's New Olympic Amphitheater and at Foley's Amphitheater. Several smaller houses—the Phoenix, the first Athenaeum, the first French Adelphi and the first of three Jenny Lind theaters—would open later in 1850. With San Francisco plagued by fires, many of these early theaters would be lost to the flames, only to be quickly rebuilt in the same spot or at a nearby location. In 1851, they would be joined by two additional theaters: the Theater of the Arts and the American. San Francisco Hall would open in 1852, followed by the Olympic Theater in 1853. Lighting in these theaters had been traditionally provided by candles or whale oil lamps. The gas-lit Metropolitan opened its doors on Christmas Day 1853 with a performance of *Richard III*, featuring Edwin Booth as Richard, wearing his late father's crown.[14]

The most frequently performed works in antebellum San Francisco were those of William Shakespeare, and the most popular was *Macbeth*.

A Western Theater for Northern & Southern Politics

The Metropolitan Theatre (center) on Montgomery near Washington Street was the first in San Francisco to feature gas lighting. Gaslight sconces flank the front entrances of the theater building. *Courtesy Library of Congress.*

Shakespeare's plays appealed to the local populace because they reflected their own ambitions and the drama and politics of the era, as his "histories and tragedies wove morals about good and evil, tyranny and freedom, that substantially formed the outlook of political figures from [David] Broderick to Abraham Lincoln."[15]

During the 1850s, "1,105 theatrical productions [were] given in San Francisco…[T]hat sum reflects 907 plays, forty-eight operas (in five different languages: Italian, French, German, Spanish, English), eighty-four extravaganzas, ballets, or pantomimes, and sixty-six minstrel shows."[16] Miners were known to toss chunks of gold onto a stage if they had especially enjoyed a particular production. Following a performance, the stage floor would be carefully swept for smaller grains of gold. Without a doubt, San Francisco was well on its way to becoming a theater town and a western theatrical counterpart to New York City.

Antebellum and Civil War San Francisco

Two particularly innovative theater entrepreneurs emerged in San Francisco. The first, Dr. David G. Robinson, formerly of Maine, had arrived in the city in 1850. He became known locally as "Yankee" Robinson. While he had had some involvement with theaters in New York, mainly as a burlesque actor, Dr. Robinson initially planned to open an apothecary on Portsmouth Square. First, however, he needed to make some fast money, and he had an interesting idea for doing just that. Robinson and his brother-in-law rented a boat and sailed out to the Farallon Islands (thirty miles outside the Golden Gate). There, they collected thousands of eggs laid by California murres (seabirds) and brought them back to the city to sell at ridiculously high prices. They netted $3,000. Robinson's portion would be his "nest egg" to finance his theatrical ambitions.[17] Later that year, he teamed up with James Evrard, a local actor, occasional female impersonator and, later, sergeant for the San Francisco police. In July 1850, they opened a two-hundred-seat theater they called the Dramatic Museum.[18] This was a small venue that tended toward comedies and musicals. A few years later, Robinson included burlesques. He would next open the Adelphi Theatre, which featured the city's first opera, and in 1851, he built the elegant American Theatre. A playwright as well, Robinson penned several plays. One was a farce about the unrealistic expectations of gold seekers called *Seeing the Elephant*. An immediate success, it was followed by two dramas: *The Reformed Drunkard* and *The Past, the Present and Future of San Francisco*, the latter being billed as "a lampoon history of the city." It turned out that Dr. Robinson's impact on San Francisco and its theaters would be short-lived. It unexpectedly ended in 1856, when "Yankee" Robinson died in Mobile, Alabama, of yellow fever caught while traveling back to the East Coast.

Robinson had a local rival in Tom Maguire, who had arrived in San Francisco from New York City in 1849 with his wife, Emma. The Maguires took in boarders, and one of their first was their friend David Broderick, who arrived in the same year and would stay with them until 1854. Down the road, Broderick would become a rich man by politically positioning himself in San Francisco, a springboard for his entering state and national politics. He would also attract significant enemies. Maguire distinguished himself in other ways. He acquired and operated the Parker House, which he turned into a magnificently outfitted hotel and gambling saloon. Maguire, who loved his plays and players, decided to add a theater to it. He built an additional level onto the Parker House and named it the Jenny Lind[19] Theatre. It featured seating for 800. The Jenny Lind, along with the Adelphi and the Dramatic Museum, was destroyed by one of two fires that occurred in the first half of 1851. Maguire's second Jenny Lind suffered the same fate in June of that year. Undaunted, he built a third just across the street from Portsmouth Square. That Jenny Lind was considered to be among the finest theaters of its day. The third Jenny Lind was built of Australian pink stone and featured a handsome light pink interior with gold gilding. Its opening play in October 1851 was *All That Glitters Is Not Gold*, and patrons streamed in to fill its 2,000 seats. The Jenny Lind presented a wide variety of plays and well-known players, including various members of the Booth family, before it was sold and, with the help of David Broderick, transformed into San Francisco's city hall. Using the proceeds, Maguire purchased San Francisco Hall, a one-story building whose theater was stage-managed by June Booth and often featured his brother Edwin. In 1856, two levels were added to the hall, which was renamed Maguire's Opera House. Its elegant interior had seating for 1,700 patrons. A lover of opera, Maguire then built the Academy of Music in 1862. He wanted it to be the city's temple of grand opera. It was, but the exorbitant costs of its lavish productions proved to be a significant drain on Maguire's financial resources.

Maguire was a showman on all levels, particularly in the local courts, where he pursued several lawsuits, including one against the *Daily Dramatic Chronicle*. He sued its proprietors, the de Young brothers,[20] for slander. They were arrested for conspiring to damage Maguire's good name and reputation through their paper's biting critiques of his productions. The de Youngs were fined five dollars, and the case was dismissed.

In 1850, a melodrama, featuring an out-of-town cast, was performed at Robinson's American Theatre. During a particularly dramatic moment, one of the actors came out onto the stage, threw out his arms and exclaimed, "What does this mean?" A member of the audience, apparently very familiar with the positioning of the arms of the semaphore up on Signal Hill used to announce arriving ships, called out, "Side-wheel steamer!" The audience burst into applause and laughter while the puzzled cast looked on, neither understanding the reference nor the response. In 1853, that semaphore was enhanced with a six-mile telegraph line, the first in California, connecting Signal Hill and Point Lobos at Land's End, west of the Golden Gate. This telegraph significantly improved communications regarding incoming ships. Signal/Semaphore Hill then became known as Telegraph Hill.

Western pioneers led the way for the profiteers. There was a saying during the gold rush era that the miners mined the mines and everyone

Antebellum and Civil War San Francisco

San Francisco's myriad theaters offered venues for lectures, political speeches and rallies and a diversity of theatrical entertainment. *Created and designed by Mary K. Ohliger.*

else mined the miners. Many miners would be relieved of the value of an entire season's gold mining efforts while wintering in San Francisco. Professional gamblers, eager to win away the miners' hard-earned gold; saloonkeepers; prostitutes; and, to some extent, actors were all in that group. But as miners discovered, so was practically everybody else in San Francisco. Costs of everything—baths, haircuts, meals, hotels, boarding houses, alcohol, services of various types—absolutely everything, were dramatically inflated. Down every block and around every corner were individuals and businesses anxious for a share of the miners' wealth. However, shopkeepers, among others, disliked dealing in the gold dust (flakes) brought in by the miners, preferring hard currency in the form of coinage. But with the country's official mint thousands of miles away in Philadelphia, who would mint the coins locally?

David Broderick and Frederick Kohler met in New York City, where Kohler had trained as a jeweler while Broderick had worked as a stonecutter, bouncer and saloonkeeper. Broderick was Irish Catholic and a native of Washington, D.C., while Kohler, of German descent, was a New York native. In addition to his various occupations, Broderick was also quite a bookworm; like Lincoln, he was self-educated. Forced to drop out of school, he made up for it by always reading, particularly focusing on the great works of English literature. An aspiring politician, Broderick also avidly studied political theory. Both he and Kohler had been volunteer firemen in New York, where Broderick recognized that fire companies were working-class social clubs and potential political organizations that could be used as stepping-stones to a political career. That experience would come in handy when both men moved west.

The two arrived in San Francisco on a cold and foggy June day in 1849. Hundreds of abandoned ships from literally all around the world greeted them, many rotting as they sat on the tidelands of Yerba Buena Cove. Broderick and Kohler weren't sure what to think as they made their way along the docks and onto the noisy and chaotic city streets. While most of their shipmates ran off to the gold fields, they both stayed behind in San Francisco and then realized that their own golden opportunity was right in front of them. With no mint as yet operating in the booming city, Kohler and Broderick formed a partnership and co-founded a business: F.D. Kohler & Company, which bought placer gold and turned it into gold coins. Financed by a start-up loan of $3,500 from Broderick's longtime New York friend Colonel Jonathan D. Stevenson, the two began striking coins with face values of five and ten dollars, effectively creating a private mint. The key to profits was that the actual gold content of these coins was approximately four and eight dollars, respectively. Business was very good and the proceeds even better. Competitors soon sprang up, and Kohler and Broderick eventually sold their business and moved on to other ventures.[21] In 1851, Congress authorized a branch mint for San Francisco. The city's first federal mint opened on Commercial Street in April 1854, and for twenty years, gold coins were minted at that site. This official mint occupied an existing building that had formerly housed the private minting firm of Curtis, Ferry & Ward, a competitor of Kohler and Broderick. That private mint had operated as the U.S. Assay Office of Gold and assayed, melted and minted gold for coins in 1852–53.

As a working-class Irishman in New York City, Broderick allied with those who viewed themselves as the victims of "white slavery" in the North. He embraced the radical politics of George Henry Evans, an Englishman who immigrated to the United States and advocated on behalf of free white labor, which, in his view, was being outrageously victimized by the wealthy. As Evans saw it, the rich industrialists in the North were enslaving the white workers in much the same way as the Southern planters did the blacks. Slavery of any kind was unpalatable to Evans, who "in his extensive writings, left no doubt that the slaveholding elite posed a serious threat to the well-being of the American Republic and that the goals and aspirations of the white working class were incompatible with slavery."[22] One significant difference was that the white "slaves" of the North voted, while the black slaves of the South did not.

Evans promoted his views beginning in the 1830s through his editing and publication of radical newspapers such as the *Working Man's Advocate*, *The Radical* and *People's Rights*. He also strongly supported the idea of the free distribution of western public lands by the federal government. Doing that, Evans believed, would attract new settlers westward, more evenly spread the nation's population and lessen the demand for jobs in the overpopulated, industrial Northeast.

Political wheeler-dealer David C. Broderick. *Courtesy Library of Congress.*

Evans's advocacy of this homesteading movement would eventually make its way into national politics and the ideology of the Free-Soil Party. Broderick would himself become a Free-Soiler as he ascended through California's political infrastructure.

The Free-Soilers were an interesting lot who joined the movement for a variety of reasons: they opposed slavery or its expansion, they detested the Southern plantation system and mores, they wanted a free homestead and/or they wanted to keep the West, particularly California, all white.

Chapter 5

The Thirty-First State

As 1850 began, thirty states comprised the United States. Fifteen were free, and fifteen were slave states. The admittance of California as a state would upset that balance either way. The proposed state's constitution continued the banishment of slavery that had first been applied in Alta California twenty years earlier, when it was still part of Mexico. Most American gold miners in California wanted that ban on slavery to be continued. Southern interests in Congress, however, fiercely disputed that ban and viewed the West as the natural place in which to expand slavery from the increasingly worn-out lands in the Southeast. Northern interests, meanwhile, believed that President Polk, a Tennessee slaveholder and an expansionist, had instigated the Mexican-American War under the guise of ultimately extending slavery to the West. Potential statehood for California would collide with the contentious issue of slavery, further fueling the already heated debate in Congress and forcing decisions.

An ongoing congressional argument centered, in part, on the Wilmot Proviso, which had been proposed by Senator David Wilmot (Pennsylvania) in 1846 and would ban slavery in any new territory acquired from Mexico (excluding Texas). Debates regarding the proviso continued as 1847 turned into 1848, and the treaty ending the war with Mexico was formally signed in February. Then, news arrived in Washington of the great gold discovery northeast of San Francisco. The stakes had risen, and so would tensions.

The November 1848 presidential election was won by Zachary Taylor, a Kentucky slaveholder and ostensibly a Whig.[23] A former Mexican-American

War general, he viewed himself as an independent, thus avoiding partisan loyalty. Among those in Washington with actual experience in the West, Taylor viewed the idea of bringing slavery to Alta California as impractical, as he felt the area could not readily support the big slave-labor crops of the time: sugar and cotton, the white gold of the South. He, along with many others, had grown tired of the long-winded, contentious congressional debates and pushed for a long-overdue resolution.

Thousands of American gold seekers, including non-slaveholding Southerners, began heading west in 1849 to a California that still had no legislative or judicial infrastructure in place. (This westward rush caused Alta California's non-tribal population to rapidly increase from approximately two thousand residents in 1848 to nearly ninety-three thousand by 1850.) Southern legislators back in Washington threatened to secede rather than apply the terms of the Wilmot Proviso. They bickered, they shouted and they called for disunion if slavery was not extended to the West. Southerners feared becoming a permanent minority in Congress and continued to argue for all of Alta California to be left open to slavery. The protracted and often bitter series of debates dragged on into 1850, with the political climate becoming increasingly polarized.

When Thomas Butler King arrived back in Washington in 1850, he found a divided Congress and a divided Whig Party. King discovered that his role as President Taylor's emissary in California had, in part, caused the Whig dissension. While Taylor and many in the Whig Party continued to support California's admission into the Union as a free state, Southern Democrats saw an opportunity to reinforce the wedge in the Whig Party. The president, for his part, reiterated his position regarding slavery in the territories. He emphasized that any decisions regarding potential statehood for California needed to originate with its residents and that it had. Taylor advised Congress to accept the decision of the people of California regarding the slavery issue that was written into its new constitution. But Southern Democrats and some Whigs remained concerned about King's role during California's constitutional convention proceedings, especially as he was one of the few Southerners who remained loyal to Taylor.

On the floor of the House, Representative Samuel Inge of Alabama declared that King was responsible for the inclusion of the antislavery clause into California's constitution and its unanimous adoption by the convention delegates. King vigorously defended himself and his actions, and many, including former governor Riley and William Gwin, a Southerner himself, defended King and confirmed his rebuttals. Eventually, the charges against

King faded away. He was vindicated when members of Congress began poring over an informative government report King had written about Alta California that detailed its mineral and agricultural resources, its soil and climate, its potential commercial development, its fledgling wine industry, its role as a market for products from the East, the likelihood of lucrative trade with the Orient and the positioning of San Francisco as a conduit for it all.[24]

Many Southerners in the Senate viewed the potential admission of California to the Union as a scheme to weaken the South and increase the coercive power of the North. If California became a state rather than a territory, Congress would not be able to impose the institution of slavery on it. A congressional compromise was drafted by Senator Henry Clay (Kentucky), who reminded Congress that it had no more right to impose slavery on California than it had to impose abolition on a slave state or to prevent slavery within the perimeters of a border state. Senator Daniel Webster (Massachusetts) backed Clay's viewpoint, while Senator John C. Calhoun (South Carolina) opposed it, warning that the Union could come apart if Southern concerns were ignored. Despite Clay's dramatic and enticing presentation, Southerners would not be moved and continued to complain of the prospect of slave states being outnumbered by free states. They feared that allowing California to enter the Union as a free state would open the doors to more free states and dissolve Southern domination of Congress.

Senator Jefferson Davis (Mississippi) led the charge against Clay's compromise. Davis proposed to simply split the state of California in half. By extending the Missouri Compromise line westward to the Pacific Coast (at 36° 30′ latitude), the southern portion could become a territory and permit slavery. Senator Calhoun added that "the admission of California [as a free state] was 'worse than the Wilmot Proviso.' It left the South with only two choices: 'submission or resistance.' And Calhoun left no doubt where he stood."[25] Neither did Jefferson Davis. In their view, the social structure of the South was in jeopardy if slavery was not permitted to expand westward.

Even while the terms of what would become known as the Compromise of 1850 were being negotiated in Congress, a local movement for the division of California, the first of many, had begun. Not wanting to be politically controlled by Northern California interests, particularly the mining interests in and around San Francisco, residents of the southern portion of California petitioned Congress for a separate designation as the Territory of Southern California. The burden of taxation, the overall size of the potential new state, the challenge of its governing and its congressional representation were all factors supporting that proposal. Meanwhile, back in Washington, Senator Henry Foote (Mississippi) advocated for dividing California at 35° 30´ latitude, sixty miles farther south than Davis's proposal. The area below this line could then be known as the Territory of Colorado, according to Foote. While his proposal was voted down, Senator Foote was one of a small group of Southern Democrats who supported Clay's compromise.

A Senator from Illinois, Stephen A. Douglas, realized that Clay's entire proposal would never make it through Congress as a single package but thought that it might make it through if voted on piece by piece. Congress's mood was changing as members on both sides were becoming exhausted and exasperated by the endless bitter debates. As was anticipated, Senator Calhoun had died at the end of March following a long illness. President Taylor unexpectedly died in early July. Douglas then joined forces with Taylor's successor, Millard Fillmore (New York), a supporter of the compromise package. A bit of maneuvering by Senator Douglas with respect to voting that took place over a six-week period sealed the deal, and Fillmore signed the various resolutions as quickly as they were approved. By successfully moving the compromise resolutions forward through both houses of Congress, Senator Douglas had achieved the seemingly unachievable. A decade later, he would be positioned as one of Abraham Lincoln's opponents during the presidential race of 1860.

California formally entered the Union on September 9, 1850, and was the first noncontiguous landmass to become a state. The next day, John C. Frémont and William M. Gwin were sworn in as California's first two senators over objections from Senator Jefferson Davis, who sought to block their admittance to Congress. Unable to gain support from fellow Southern legislators, who sought harmony, at least for the moment, Davis's motion failed. Together, Frémont and Gwin represented the only state to join the Union that had not previously been a territory except for the original thirteen colonies and Texas, which had been an independent country.

President Fillmore rewarded Thomas Butler King for his past efforts by appointing him tax collector for the port of San Francisco. He would work and live at the customhouse at Portsmouth Square. King did earn his keep by consistently supporting the alliance between government and business in the growing city.

In mid-October, the *Oregon* sailed through the Golden Gate, sporting banners declaring that "California Is a State" and officially bringing the news of statehood to San Francisco. An Admission's Day celebration— the first—took place in Portsmouth Square on October 29 and included attaching a paper star, the thirty-first, to an existing flag that was then run up the pole. Statehood had finally been achieved.

Two San Francisco residents, Frémont and Gwin, initially represented California in the Senate. Frémont was unable to win reelection, however, mainly because he was an outspoken Free-Soiler but also due to issues regarding his *Las Mariposas* property in California. Moreover, the 1850 Compromise had polarized California politics, and the state's South-leaning legislature wasn't keen on Frémont at that point. Seeing an opportunity, Thomas Butler King traveled to San José to again promote himself for a Senate seat. For a time, victory seemed within reach, but as one legislative ballot after another was taken, 141 in all, no candidate emerged as a winner.

An artist's rendering of the October 1850 Admission's Day parade at Montgomery and California Streets. Signal (Telegraph) Hill rises in the background. *Courtesy Library of Congress.*

The legislature adjourned until January 1, 1852, when it would try again. King returned to San Francisco a disappointed man.

For the next nine months, California would be represented in Congress by only one senator: William Gwin. These circumstances put Gwin solely in charge of overseeing the staffing of federal positions in California with veto power over those appointments. To no one's surprise, the vast majority of these posts would come to be staffed with Southerners (i.e., postmasters, naval officers, appraisers, federal attorneys and treasurers, revenue officials, lighthouse keepers and inspectors). Southerners of lesser means staffed the land office, the Indian office and San Francisco's customhouse, so many that the latter was labeled by David Broderick as the "Virginia Poor

Former Georgia representative Thomas Butler King failed in his quests to become a California senator. *Courtesy Library of Congress.*

House." Broderick was aware that Northerners were being discriminated against, and he fought back by becoming involved with administering state patronage, often offered to those who had been unable to get the coveted federal jobs. Nonetheless, Gwin's favoritism of Southerners continued. Thanks to the politics of the era, Gwin had unexpectedly found himself in an advantageous position, and he made the most of it. Gwin would remain in control of federal patronage throughout much of the decade, while his appointments and those who reported to them were all beholden to him. Questions about Gwin's management of these patronage appointments led to an argument with California congressman Joseph McCorkle (Ohio), which, in turn, led to a duel. Fortunately, Gwin and McCorkle each fired shots that missed.

William Gwin was criticized throughout the South for having agreed to the provision that California apply for entry to the Union as a free state during the drafting of California's new constitution in Monterey in 1849. Gwin's position was that he did what he had to do to ultimately become a senator. He was a realist, but Southerners would have none of that. They viewed California's admittance as a free state as jeopardizing Southern domination of the Senate and the expansion of slavery into the West. There were again calls for the new thirty-first state to be split at the $36°\ 30'$ or $35°\ 30'$ line of latitude. It was a viewpoint that was also debated in the California state legislature. David Broderick had been elected to the California state senate and in 1851 became president of that body. He was then positioned to kill every bill and every legislative maneuver that included potentially bringing slavery to California and/or splitting the state. In San Francisco, the *Daily Alta California* in 1852 aggressively spoke out against both state division and any proposed constitutional conventions to formally address the matter.

A Western Theater for Northern & Southern Politics

In November 1851, John Weller was elected as California's newest senator, succeeding John Frémont. He took office in 1852 and served through 1857. Though from Ohio, Weller had married into a slave-owning family in Virginia and had developed a Southern perspective. His election meant that California was at that point actually represented by two senators with Southern proclivities who, in practice, never really threatened the South's hold on the Senate. Both Gwin and Weller would maintain their respective plantation holdings and the slaves attached to them.

November 2, 1852, marked the first presidential election in which California voters participated. In San Francisco, 36 percent of eligible voters were from the Middle Atlantic States, primarily New York. New England and the South each contributed 20 percent of local eligible voters, while 18 percent were foreign-born and 6 percent were from the Midwest.[26] All three presidential candidates represented Northern states. The incumbent president, Millard Fillmore, was passed over by his own party (Whig) in favor of General Winfield Scott, who was running from New Jersey but was actually a native Virginian. Franklin Pierce of New Hampshire was chosen as the Democratic candidate, while John P. Hale, also a New Hampshire native, represented the Free-Soil faction. Pierce won handily with 254 electoral votes, including all 4 of California's. The 1852 election would be the last hurrah for the Whig Party, which collapsed shortly thereafter due to national tensions related mainly to the slavery issue.

As the antebellum era transitioned into the Civil War years, five additional states were admitted, all as free states: Minnesota (1858), Oregon (1859), Kansas (1861), West Virginia (1863) and Nevada (1864). The equilibrium that congressional Southerners had fought so hard to maintain during debates over California statehood had moved beyond their grasp.

Chapter 6

Leading Players: New Englanders, New Yorkers and Southerners

Seeking refuge in the West, about 238 Mormons sailed around the Horn on the *Brooklyn* in mid-1846. Leading the group was Samuel Brannan, a Mormon elder at the tender age of twenty-six. Upon arrival in Yerba Buena, the Maine native was dismayed to see the American flag rather than the Mexican flag, which he had expected, flying over Portsmouth Square. (When anti-Mormonism pushed them out of New York and Ohio, Mormons planned to relocate to the hopefully more tolerant Mexican Alta California.) Having left the United States only to inadvertently sail right back into it, Brannan decided to stay, and these Mormon newcomers tripled the population of Yerba Buena. The majority consisted of artisans and craftsmen and included a blacksmith, a saddle maker and an apothecarian along with "bakers, surveyors, coopers, gunsmiths, masons, carpenters and cabinetmakers, cobblers, tanners, tailors, a brewer, a cigar maker, a silversmith, a watchmaker, a weaver and several attorneys at law."[27] Brannan brought his own entrepreneurial skills as well and proved to be a colorful figure in a town destined to be full of colorful figures. After initially dismissing the supposed discovery of gold, it was he who confirmed the rumors in May 1848 by marching around Portsmouth Square carrying a gold-filled container while shouting, "Gold! Gold! Gold from the American River!" Brannan's town crier–like proclamation created a frenzy that resulted in a stampede up to the gold fields. Brannan knew there was money to be made and potentially lots of it. He had shrewdly made his announcement after he had already filled warehouses in the city and his two shops near the American River with the wares he thought a potential gold miner might require. Brannan reportedly bought up all the miner's pans he could find for twenty cents apiece and then resold them for fifteen dollars each. He was only too happy to sell any and all items gold seekers needed, wanted and demanded, and he reaped incredible profits doing so. Brannan enjoyed a steady flow of customers and, thanks to them, was one of the first millionaires in California.

Sam Brannan also founded the city's first newspaper, the *California Star*, in January 1847, printed on a press he had brought with him on the *Brooklyn*. It was a four-page weekly that featured articles in English and Spanish. The *Star*'s masthead declared that the paper was "Devoted to the Liberties and Interests of the People of California." It was in practice a forum against the domination of the military government. Dr. Elbert B. Jones, a fellow Mormon, would briefly serve as editor. Jones was succeeded by Edward Kemble, the nineteen-year-old typesetter for the *Star*. Kemble was a native of upstate New York and a non-Mormon who was interested in journalism and politics. He had sailed westbound on the *Brooklyn* with Brannan's group for adventures in Alta California and to help run a newspaper.

Aware of growing discontent in the gold fields related to slavery issues, Brannan, who disliked slavery, used his newspaper as his forum for declaring in favor of an all-white California. In January 1849, Brannan publicly voiced his views at a meeting in Sacramento. The presiding officer, future governor Peter Burnett, backed Brannan. The resolution for an all-white California passed easily, as it would again a month later during a public meeting in San Francisco. In what was a miners' economy, Brannan claimed that more than 90 percent of California residents backed him. Miners simply did not want to compete with slavery in the mines and, in April 1849, drafted a code that included limiting "the size of a mining claim to what one man could work by himself. They also elected a committee of the oldest miners to enforce it."[28] The miners' code applied to anyone who brought slaves to the gold fields. It was harshly enforced with punishments that ranged from cutting off body parts to hangings. Later that year, the issue of slaves and free blacks in California would be formally addressed by delegates at the Constitutional Convention in Monterey.

The *California Star* published until June 1848, when its entire staff ran off to the gold fields. Brannan's paper encountered some competition when the operations for the *Californian*, an older publication founded in Monterey in 1846, were moved up to San Francisco in mid-1847. Brannan decided to sell the *California Star* to Edward Kemble for $800. Kemble merged the

Sam Brannan and the *California Star* office. Brannan proved to be the dynamic bridge between the sleepy pueblo of Yerba Buena and thriving city of San Francisco. *Mural by Anton Refregier, Rincon Annex Post Office. Courtesy Library of Congress.*

Star with the *Californian*, which he by then also owned. The new, combined publication was named the *Daily Alta California*, the first daily newspaper in California. In October 1849, its printing press would be used to print copies of the proposed California constitution. The newspaper proved to be profitable but suffered two setbacks in the early 1850s. First, a great fire swept through the city in June 1851, completely burning out the paper's offices. That calamity was followed a year later by the unexpected death of Kemble's good friend, business partner and now congressman, Edward Gilbert. Gilbert was the losing participant in a duel, dying of his wounds at the age of thirty. He had been the *Alta*'s editor and had served as a San Francisco delegate to the 1849 California Constitutional Convention, reporting on its proceedings for the newspaper. Disheartened, Kemble sold the *Daily Alta California* and left San Francisco.[29]

Brannan served on San Francisco's first city council and in 1853 was elected to the State Senate. In 1858, he built the Seal Rock House, nestled in San Francisco's western cliffs overlooking the Pacific Ocean. It predated the first Cliff House by five years. Ever the entrepreneur, he developed banks, telegraph companies and railroads throughout the state, becoming increasingly wealthy. Brannan would eventually own one-fifth of San Francisco's real estate and one-fourth of Sacramento's.

When former U.S. consul Thomas Larkin (Massachusetts) realized that Monterey would likely remain a provincial Spanish/Mexican town, he moved his family to the vibrant city of San Francisco in 1853. Larkin built the first brick building in the city, a resplendent three-story residence with extensive gardens on Stockton Street. From his Montgomery Street office, Larkin would manage his extensive real estate holdings and advocate for statewide and national railroads. He grew wealthy, but his time grew short when he contracted typhoid fever and died at fifty-six.

Lieutenant William Tecumseh Sherman (Ohio) traveled west from New York around the Horn aboard the USS *Lexington*. While on board, he became acquainted with Lieutenant Henry W. Halleck. Both had been

Thomas Larkin's burial site in Cypress Lawn Cemetery in Colma, California. He died in 1858 in his San Francisco home on Stockton Street near Pacific Avenue. *Courtesy of the author.*

called west due to the Mexican-American War. They arrived in Yerba Buena in July 1847, two days before the name changed to San Francisco. Shortly after arriving, they encountered Captain Joseph Folsom, who had been a classmate of Sherman's at West Point. Folsom was then chief quartermaster. Sherman settled into San Francisco performing war-related administrative duties. In 1848, he rode to Monterey, meeting with Colonel Richard Mason, then military governor. Sherman accompanied Mason to the American River region to confirm the rumors of the gold discovery. They would be joined en route by Captain Folsom and a few other soldiers. Governor Mason would not believe the rumors and stories about the gold discovery until he saw it for himself. Both he and Sherman collected flakes and nuggets to send to President Polk along with a report drafted by Sherman about the discovery. It would all arrive in Washington by November, prompting the president's official public announcement. Sherman himself profited from his early knowledge about the gold find by investing in one of Sam Brannan's stores as a silent partner and by hiring himself out as a surveyor, a skill he had learned at West Point. He participated in surveying the site that would eventually become the city of Sacramento. He then returned to Monterey, where he attended the constitutional convention at Colton Hall. Sherman temporarily resigned from the military in 1853 to take on the duties of managing a downtown bank in San Francisco.

John Frémont had made a name for himself throughout the 1840s exploring the West on various expeditions, earning the sobriquet "Pathfinder of the West." His wife, Jessie, had meanwhile remained on the East Coast. The two would be reunited in San Francisco during the summer of 1849. Mrs. Frémont and her six-year-old daughter, Lily, arrived on the *Panama* in June, docking at the Long Wharf. They were taken to Tom Maguire's Parker House overlooking Portsmouth Square, where they would reside in comfort while waiting for Colonel Frémont to arrive. Always eager to discuss politics, Jessie filled her time dispelling or confirming the many rumors about goings-on in Congress and at the Zachary Taylor White House.

Born in her mother's family's manor house near Lexington, Virginia, Jessie was well educated for her time and frequently traveled with her father, Senator Thomas Hart Benton, who represented Missouri in Congress for thirty years. Those experiences would shape her, as she was regularly exposed to political, economic and social dynamics in Virginia, Washington and St. Louis. John was a junior army officer when they met and married. Together, they would write bestselling stories of John's western expeditions, making him and his scout, Kit Carson, famous. Those stories inspired many to make the journey westward and were often used as guides for the trip. The stories also promoted the idea of Manifest Destiny. When the world went to California in the late 1840s, the Frémonts did as well, and they would live in San Francisco, Monterey and Mariposa throughout the 1850s. Jessie brought her political savvy and her growing opposition to slavery with her. She strongly influenced her husband, John, a Southerner raised in Charleston, South Carolina; he turned against slavery and its expansion to the West. With John often traveling, Jessie settled into San Francisco society and was always ready and willing to participate in discussions about the important issues of the day. Jessie would play an active role in the anti-secession movement in California.

William Gwin arrived in San Francisco in June 1849, nine days before David Broderick. Shortly thereafter, Gwin would have his first encounter with Broderick, the Northerner who would become his greatest rival for political power.

Following his foray into speculative coin production, Broderick used his profits to speculate in waterfront properties in San Francisco and made a fortune. Broderick soon realized that there was an even greater fortune to be had in gaining political power. From his years in New York, he knew that one way of attaining it was in hooking up with the local volunteer fire companies. Doing the same thing in San Francisco gave Broderick more than a few opportunities to distinguish himself as a fearless firefighter alongside the other volunteers. Much admired for their bravery, these volunteer firefighters were perfectly positioned to get out the vote for upcoming elections. Broderick encouraged this and, along with some behind-the-scenes partners, created a political machine in San Francisco, initially financing it with his own money. Local elected officeholders in those days were generally compensated with various fees they collected in the course of doing their jobs rather than set salaries. Broderick offered them the backing of his local Democratic machine in exchange for half those fees, an arrangement that led him to control San Francisco politics within his first year in San Francisco and finance his winning campaign for state senator. Having mastered the lessons of New York–style Tammany politics and strategies, Broderick worked assiduously to institute the Tammany system of organization into San Francisco and statewide politics.

No less than six significant fires would destroy all or part of San Francisco between 1849 and 1851. Some were accidental; many were arson. But all were destructive to local residents and businesses. The first occurred on Christmas Eve 1849 at Dennison's Exchange Saloon,[30] which had been acquired earlier that month by a Southerner, Thomas Bartell. There was a custom at the time in San Francisco that a black man could be served one drink in a saloon generally patronized by whites, but only one drink. Bartell did not subscribe to the custom, and when a black man entered Dennison's and ordered a drink, Bartell responded by beating him senseless. The black man swore revenge. At dawn on the twenty-fourth, a fire began that burned down Dennison's and about fifty surrounding buildings. Broderick and Kohler were among the first volunteer firemen on the scene. Broderick's heroics, in particular, steered him toward winning a seat in the state senate. By the spring of 1851, he had become senate president pro tempore.

Over the next few years, the city seemed to alternate between burning and rebuilding. The fifth of these great fires, occurring in early May 1851, was particularly devastating, destroying almost the entire city. The Frémonts were among those who lost their homes. Despite the valiant efforts of the firefighters, approximately two thousand buildings burned, including the

Broderick's Empire #1 engine company, organized in June 1850 and shown here with its doors open, was located on Sacramento Street. *Courtesy San Francisco History Center, San Francisco Public Library.*

customhouse, an important collection and storage site of much-needed revenue for the city. Rebuilding was once again immediately underway.

Such was the scene that greeted a young girl when she arrived with her parents on the *Tennessee* that sailed into Yerba Buena Cove on May 20, 1851. Among its passengers was a Dr. Charles Hitchcock, an army surgeon who had graduated from West Point. The army had reassigned him to California, naming him medical director of the Pacific Coast. Dr. Hitchcock traveled west via the Isthmus of Panama, accompanied by his wife, Martha, and their seven-year-old daughter, Lillie. As the *Tennessee* docked, the family was greeted by two close friends of Dr. Hitchcock's from his days at West Point: Captains Henry Halleck and Joseph Folsom.

The Hitchcock family found Yerba Buena Cove filled with hundreds of abandoned ships. Throngs of people and a dozen dogs crowded their wharf, moving amid the piles of barrels, boxes and trunks, as the Hitchcocks looked on from the deck of the *Tennessee*. Barkers shouted, the dogs yelped, babies cried and at least one street evangelist harangued the mainly disinterested crowd roaming about. The Hitchcocks, astounded by the sights and sounds of San Francisco and not particularly impressed, warily disembarked into this unexpected madness and followed Halleck and Folsom to a boardinghouse at Stockton and Washington Streets, an area that had managed to survive the recent conflagration. There, they would encounter some of San Francisco's most prominent residents, including then-senator William Gwin and soon-to-be-senator John Weller. For little Lillie, the Hitchcock family's journey west and their arrival in San Francisco was all a continuous great adventure. Then, within a month, just as she and her family were settling in, another fire broke out, destroying their Stockton Street boardinghouse along with other structures in the immediate area. Lillie's family would manage to save the bulk of their possessions and clothing but needed a new place to live. They temporarily moved in with Captain Folsom, who lived in an elegant home on Rincon Hill, an area south of Market Street that was mainly owned by him. Captain Folsom, well established in the city by the time the Hitchcock family arrived, was already counted among the city's wealthiest men, in large part due to his real estate holdings. Captain Folsom also owned the Tehama House hotel, among whose intermittent guests during 1852–54 was future Civil War general Ulysses S. Grant.

Lillie Hitchcock had been born at West Point in 1843. She grew up in the North, the South and the West, as her father's work and her mother's ambitions caused them to move frequently. Lillie's father, Charles, was from Maryland, while her mother, Martha Hunter, hailed from a plantation in

North Carolina. Upon arrival in the city, the Hitchcocks found that much of the top echelon of San Francisco society consisted of Southerners. These Southerners were part of the Southern aristocracy who had moved to San Francisco to enhance their wealth or further their careers. They would come to be known as the Chivalry Southerners or "Chivs." The Chivs would find their local adversaries in the Shovelry Northerners, most of whom were working-class people with jobs that required manual labor.

Residential hotels were very popular in 1850s San Francisco among those who could afford them. The appeal of these establishments was that they featured servants, clean linens daily and good, quality meals several times a day. Residential guests came and went as they pleased, while having all their needs attended to and bearing little responsibility besides paying their weekly hotel bills and taking care not to accidentally burn down the place. These hotels were particularly appealing to the countless unmarried men who had relocated to San Francisco, many of whom used them as excuses for avoiding marriage and subsequently setting up their own households. They were also a refuge of sorts for women of high moral character, such as Martha Hitchcock, and their children, protecting them from the precarious and coarse streets of the city, populated with so many seemingly questionable characters, foreign and domestic. The Hitchcock family relocated to the Oriental Hotel. Mrs. Hitchcock then talked the editor of the *Daily Alta California* into allowing her to write for the newspaper. The environments of hotel residency combined with antebellum dynamics in the bustling gold rush city would give her more than enough material to write about.

Joseph Folsom, a New Hampshire native, arrived in San Francisco in 1847 with Stevenson's Regiment, a group of New York volunteers commanded by Colonel Jonathan Stevenson with ambitions to fight in the Mexican-American War. After finishing its military obligation, the regiment disbanded. Stevenson remained in the city, funding Broderick and Kohler's private minting operation. Folsom also remained in San Francisco and quietly began buying up real estate. He came to own much of the land in the area south of Market Street, including the portion covered with miners' tents that sardonically became known as "Happy Valley." Folsom also had an interest in the American Theatre on Sansome Street, the first brick structure built on the tidelands. Lillie Hitchcock was among his invited guests in October 1851 for the theater's opening night production of *The Peer and the Peasant*. She was one of the few females and very few children present in the elegant two-thousand-seat theater. While the audience deemed the opening night performances a success, the theater's owners (which also included Dr.

Robinson) had other concerns. As Martha Hitchcock reported in her "City Intelligence" column in the following day's paper, during the course of the evening's performance, the packed theater had sunk two inches into the sandy landfill upon which it had been built. Nonetheless, the theater became a popular venue.

Folsom doted on little Lillie, and they became friends despite their considerable age difference. The Hitchcock family and much of San Francisco was shocked to learn that Joseph Folsom had unexpectedly died of kidney failure during a visit to Mission San José in 1855. He was just thirty-eight years old. A town he developed in Sacramento County and had named Granite City was renamed Folsom in his honor.

During the 1850s, San Francisco grew more and more dependent on its fourteen-steam-engine fire companies and the volunteers who staffed them. Lillie Hitchcock first came into direct contact with one of these companies, the Knickerbocker #5 Fire Company, a few months after arriving in San Francisco when she herself was caught up in a fire that started in a half-finished building she was exploring. She was grateful to be saved and befriended the volunteer firemen who had responded to the alarm. Martha Hitchcock, a bona fide Southern belle, was none too pleased when her daughter, Lillie, was nicknamed "fire belle" and became a mascot for the Knickerbocker #5. Mrs. Hitchcock was further dismayed when she discovered that its members were all from New York. Dr. Hitchcock was at first amused by Lillie's new fascination but then later became very alarmed when Lillie chased after Knickerbocker's horse-drawn steam engine as it made its way up to Telegraph Hill to put out a fire. It proved impossible for the Hitchcocks to keep Lillie away from fires and the members of the Knickerbocker crew, and she remained supportive of firefighters throughout her life. Fierce political rivalries eventually forced the disbandment of the volunteer companies. (In 1866, the official San Francisco Fire Department, consisting of paid members, was formed. Two years later, Lillie Hitchcock became Mrs. Howard Coit.)

The *Oregon* sailed back into San Francisco on April 7, 1852, and among its passengers were a Scottish man, Thomas Bell, and a black woman, Mary Ellen Pleasant. Pleasant's origins were murky, and she did and said little in the way of clarification. Some said she had been born in Georgia and was an escaped slave. Others whispered that Pleasant was actually the daughter of a voodoo priestess and the youngest son of a former governor of Virginia. In her later life, Pleasant often stated that she had been born in Philadelphia. Nonetheless, her apparent mixed heritage allowed her to often pass as white.

Known for her extraordinary cooking skills, Pleasant ran a number of high-end men's dining establishments in San Francisco, where she met many of the city's movers and shakers. She gleaned bits and pieces of local gossip and valuable financial information from them as she and her staff moved about the dining rooms. Pleasant and Thomas Bell became partners, lovers and eventually millionaires as they speculated in mining, real estate and banking interests. Pleasant also invested in laundries, dairies and restaurants. She ran boardinghouses and brothels and regularly bought and sold property throughout San Francisco. Not only was she growing wealthy, but she was also positioning herself for her future endeavors. When Thomas Bell was named as a director of William Ralston's powerful Bank of California, Pleasant became Bell's silent confidante.

Mary Ellen Pleasant continually worked to improve the lives of blacks in San Francisco and in the United States. In 1858, she and her husband, John, traveled northeast to Chatham, Ontario, where they connected with Ohio abolitionist John Brown. Mrs. Pleasant actively supported Brown with both her money[31] and her presence in the South in 1859. When Brown was arrested in October following his unsuccessful raid on the Federal arsenal in Harpers Ferry, Virginia, a note from Pleasant signed with the initials "MEP" was found in his pocket. These initials were at first misread as "WEP," allowing Pleasant time to quickly and quietly slip away.

Sixteen of the twenty eucalyptus saplings that Mary Ellen Pleasant planted along Octavia Street can be seen in this westerly view of the Bell/Pleasant estate; just six eucalyptus trees remain today. *Courtesy San Francisco History Center, San Francisco Public Library.*

Also in Virginia was John Wilkes Booth. Wearing a borrowed uniform, he had temporarily joined the Richmond Grays, assigned to guard the captured Brown. Booth remained in Harpers Ferry until December and was a witness to Brown's hanging.

Mrs. Pleasant returned to San Francisco in 1861. Once back in the city, she was the conduit for the western terminus of the Underground Railroad safe house network. Pleasant would place escaped slaves as workers in the homes of San Francisco's wealthy and elite, which gave her a unique opportunity to keep abreast of goings-on among the upper classes. She also continued to fight for racial equality and against the imposition of Jim Crow practices, which had followed blacks to San Francisco and the West. In 1863, blacks finally won the right to testify against non-blacks in the state courts.

Blacks in California dated back to the Mexican era, when free blacks and escaped slaves made their way west. This population continued to grow until more and more whites began arriving, and blacks, along with American Indians and Mexicans, were subjected to physical assaults and abject discrimination during the race for golden riches. Blacks then began moving to Sacramento and San Francisco Counties, which, by 1860, contained approximately one-third of California's black population. In 1853, they founded an educational and cultural center called the San Francisco Athenaeum Institute, which included a library that contained eight hundred volumes. Also established were several churches and private schools and a newspaper called the *Mirror of the Times*. Blacks sought means by which to improve their status with respect to housing, education and basic civil and political rights and "convened the first Convention of the Colored Citizens of the State of California in 1855."[32]

In 1858, an issue arose that shook black Californians. It revolved around a black slave, Archy Lee, who had been brought to Sacramento by his owner's son, Charles Stovall, and hired out for wages. Lee learned that California was actually a free state, in which slavery was illegal. When he discovered that Stovall planned to take him back to Mississippi, Lee ran away, taking refuge with local blacks. A series of legal maneuvers then began to either release Lee to Stovall or to free Lee and allow him to remain in the West. Mary Ellen Pleasant was one of the individuals who raised funds to cover Lee's legal fees. The case worked its way up to the California Supreme Court, and sitting on that court was none other than Chief Justice David Terry and Justice Peter Burnett, the former governor. The court ruled against Lee and in favor of Stovall. An attempt by Stovall to sneak Archy Lee out of San Francisco on the steamship *Orizaba*[33] was foiled by the local police, who carried a warrant signed by local district judges for Stovall's arrest for kidnapping. A rowboat carrying Stovall and Lee pulled up alongside the *Orizaba* as it sailed toward the Golden Gate. Passengers aboard the ship were split on the Stovall/Lee issue, and in the mêlée that followed, several tried to keep the police from retrieving Lee, while others tried to get Lee on board. After a struggle, the police were at last able to get a hold of Lee and bring him back to San Francisco. More legal proceedings followed, with well-known local attorney Edward Baker speaking on behalf of Lee. A federal court finally ruled in Archy Lee's favor in late 1858. Pleasant secreted Lee in her home until things calmed down and likely assisted his retreat to Canada shortly thereafter.

By 1860, blacks represented 1 percent of the population of California, i.e., 4,000 out of 400,000 residents, the largest amount of black residents in any state or territory west of the Rockies. Overall, blacks in 1850s and '60s San Francisco were far better off than their counterparts in the East but were still subjected to the common discriminatory practices of the mid-nineteenth century. Despite lacking basic civil rights, such as not being able to vote or testify on their own behalf in court cases involving whites, the city's black community enjoyed resources of money, education and a relatively high literacy rate. Two newspapers for the black community began publishing in the city during the Civil War years: the *Pacific Appeal* (1862–80) and the *Elevator* (1865–1904), whose motto was "Equality Before the Law." Both were edited by the black journalist Philip Bell, who used both papers in his campaign against discrimination on streetcars and in the schools.

Blacks who came to San Francisco worked as sailors, cooks, maids or other laborers. Notwithstanding obstacles often created by Southern Democrats in the area, more than a few blacks would come to own successful businesses in the city, such as laundries, barbershops, real estate agencies and livery stables. Local blacks simultaneously worked for their livelihoods and futures and also for their rights and standing in the community. Buoyed by local Republican influences, San Francisco was among the first American cities to desegregate its (horse-drawn) streetcar system in 1864. However, despite a district court ruling, local drivers often wouldn't pick up blacks waiting at streetcar stops. In 1866, Mary Ellen Pleasant successfully sued the North Beach and Mission Railroad company for passing by waiting black patrons. The case dragged on for several years but was finally won when the California Supreme Court ruled in her favor. It was an important victory, as many black women, including Mrs. Pleasant, regularly used the streetcars to get to their jobs and take care of their personal business.

Chapter 7

Illicit Acts

Not everyone in gold rush–era San Francisco was enchanted with the eclectic mix of individuals roaming about the city. Several white Northerners, who had been unsuccessful in the mines, formed an anti-foreigner group that became known as the "Hounds." They were joined by disbanded members of Stevenson's New York Regiment. Their home base was a large tent called Tammany Hall. Initially, the Hounds were hired by businessmen such as Joseph Folsom to round up runaway sailors. While they could collect twenty-five dollars for each sailor who was returned to his ship, the task proved to be far easier said than done. Turning their attention to other local opportunities, they began to hound foreign miners out of the city, particularly those who had been successful. Chilean miners were favorite targets. The Hounds would demand money from these miners and then beat them and steal their property if payments were not promptly made. Led by Sam Roberts, these Hounds came to number around one hundred and were among the city's toughest characters. They became an intimidating gang that not only robbed and killed foreign miners but also looted and burned local stores and demanded protection money. Animosities between Anglos and *Californios* were not unknown at the time and often extended to miners from South America. City officials generally looked the other way, but as the Hounds went to extremes, a call for action arose.

One day, a large group of Hounds descended upon the offices of the *Daily Alta California*, raising havoc and demanding that the paper cease printing articles and editorials against them. They suggested that an accidental fire could start in the paper's printing facility. In July 1849, concerned citizens, including Sam Brannan, assembled in Portsmouth Square to speak out against them. About 230 men were recruited to form a voluntary police force and managed to round up a pack of Hounds, about 20 of the worst offenders. Since no jail existed at the time, they were held on an anchored ship in the cove, the *Warren*, to await their trial. A young local attorney and Southerner (Georgia) by the name of Matthew Hall McAllister acted as chief prosecutor. McAllister was assisted by Frances Lippitt, while Myron Norton appeared for the accused. William Gwin served as a judge.[34] Sam Roberts and 9 of the Hounds were successfully prosecuted and banished from San Francisco. Observing the proceedings was the newly arrived David Broderick, who got his first good look at William Gwin.

In 1851, a new group arose in San Francisco consisting, in part, of released prisoners from Australia's penal colony at Botany Bay. They became known as the Sydney Ducks and were accused of a myriad of crimes, including robbery, arson and looting. Once again, Sam Brannan spoke up, calling for public hangings of the miscreants. The 1851 Vigilance Committee was formed, attracting seven hundred members, and the first Duck was hanged in early June. Thousands converged on Portsmouth Square for a rally following the hanging. They included an appalled David Broderick, who successfully dispelled the crowd with his impassioned speech denouncing the actions of the committee and calling it a band of midnight murderers. But the 1851 Committee of Vigilance, backed by an editorial in the *Daily Alta California*, won in the end. It became the de facto police force, controlling and patrolling the city. Three more Ducks were hanged that summer. Following that, the committee faded out but never formally dissolved.

In 1854, Sam Roberts was back again and attracted a new group of followers. Among their targets were members of David Broderick's Irish political machine, along with the large German contingent in San Francisco. Roberts allied with the local chapter of the national American Party in San Francisco, which was better known as the Know-Nothing Party. The party had originated in the 1840s in response to the influx of Irish and German immigrants. Its membership was limited to Protestant males, most of whom were anti-immigrant and anti-Catholic. Outsiders called them Know-Nothings.

Then, who should pop up in San Francisco but Henry Foote. The former senator from Mississippi had defeated Jefferson Davis in a run for governor of that state in 1852, running on a Unionist platform. As governor, Foote became dismayed at the anti-Union fervor in Mississippi. He resigned and

A Western Theater for Northern & Southern Politics

Left: This statue was placed by the San Francisco Bar Association in 1904. The inscription on its granite base reads: "Hall McAllister, Leader of the California Bar, Learned, Able, Eloquent, A Fearless Advocate, A Courteous Foe." *Courtesy of the author*.

Below: The 1851 Vigilance Committee hanged a Sydney "Duck" on the Market Street Wharf. *Courtesy Library of Congress*.

headed west in 1854 to set up a law practice. Within six months of his arrival, Foote was involved in local politics and aligned himself with the Know-Nothing Party. Foote helped many party candidates win seats in the state legislature. He was himself endorsed for a California senate seat that would have put him back in Congress. Local schemers, led by David Broderick, found ways to keep the California state legislature from meeting, which kept Henry Foote from being elected. It was a clever tactic and a successful one.

In California, the Know-Nothing Party quickly expanded statewide and attracted enough followers to hold a convention in Sacramento in the summer of 1855. The party won a significant number of seats in the state legislature and had backed the 1854 election of Stephen P. Webb (Massachusetts) as mayor of San Francisco. The split of the Democratic Party in California led to the Know-Nothing Party's gubernatorial victory of 1856, electing J. Neely Johnson (Indiana) as governor. The party itself rapidly declined following the 1856 election, bitterly divided over the issue of slavery, as had been the Whig Party. Henry Foote left San Francisco after the 1856 election, returning to Mississippi.

Chapter 8

The Next Act

Halleck's Folly, the Washington Block or, as it was more commonly known, the Montgomery Block, was one of the earliest significant buildings to be constructed in San Francisco. Completed in 1853, it was San Francisco's first fireproof and earthquake-resistant structure, important considerations in a city plagued by both. Dr. Hitchcock's friend Henry Halleck built the Montgomery Block to be the largest office building in the West and the tallest in San Francisco. After resigning from the army in 1854, Halleck joined the law firm of Peachy and Billings, bringing along Joseph Folsom as a client. Halleck then moved the renamed firm of Halleck, Peachy and Billings into the Block. The Bank Exchange & Billiard Saloon and retail shops filled the Block's first level, while the upper floors housed offices for lawyers, engineers, judges and businessmen, plus the relocated offices of the *Daily Alta California*.

Halleck, Peachy and Billings quickly became one of the leading law firms in San Francisco. Frederick Billings was a Northerner from Vermont and one of the first lawyers to begin practice in San Francisco shortly after his arrival in 1849. Billings met Halleck through the latter's work as a legal advisor to Governor Mason and General Riley in Monterey when Halleck served as the military secretary of California. Archibald C. Peachy, who also arrived in the city in 1849, was a Southerner from an old, aristocratic family in Williamsburg, Virginia.

Offices for the *Daily Evening Bulletin*, founded by James King of William (Virginia), were also located at the Montgomery Block beginning in 1855.

Completed in 1853, the Montgomery Block stood on Montgomery and Washington Streets until 1959. The Transamerica Pyramid building has occupied the site since the early 1970s. *Courtesy Library of Congress.*

King, who had been a member of the 1851 Vigilance Committee, had since become a self-appointed social reformer and a supporter of California justice and Southerner David Terry. On May 4, 1856, King would be shot on the street in front of the Block, a result of his editorializing against certain San Francisco residents. David Broderick, whom King denounced as a virtual dictator of the city, was one of his frequent targets; County Supervisor James P. Casey was another. Casey had been a beneficiary of Broderick's political connections and espoused his views in the *Weekly Sunday Times*, his own relatively small publication. King and Casey were engaged in a running feud and used their respective newspapers as their forums. When King wrote that Casey had been recruited to stuff ballot boxes and also revealed that he had served time in Sing-Sing Prison in New York for grand larceny, Casey was outraged. Failing to get a retraction, Casey accosted King outside the front doors of the Montgomery Block, drawing his revolver. This wasn't to be an impromptu duel but rather an outright assassination. King had little opportunity to do anything and was shot point-blank in the chest. He died a slow death, sixteen days later, in the *Bulletin*'s second-floor offices. He was thirty-four.

King's untimely death contributed to the rapid reorganization of the Vigilance Committee, which captured Casey from the local jail and then promptly hanged him and one other prisoner two days later. This 1856 Vigilance Committee had 1,500 immediate sign-ups and would grow to 5,000 members. Its revamped motto included a large all-seeing eye, presumably watching over San Francisco. June Booth was among those who signed on, and it was through the committee that he met and became friends with Lafayette C. Baker (New York). Exposure to vigilante justice in the West prepared Baker for military intelligence service in the East during the Civil War. In 1865, he would lead the pursuit for June's brother, the assassin of President Lincoln.

Frank Leslie's Illustrated Newspaper featured this drawing depicting the assassination of James King of William by James Casey at the corner of Montgomery and Washington Streets (July 19, 1856 edition). *Courtesy San Francisco History Center, San Francisco Public Library.*

The committee enjoyed its newly reactivated power while ignoring all local authority other than its own. The vigilantes became insurrectionists, pursuing Broderick and his Democratic machine and, particularly, his Irish supporters, many of whom were involved with local or state politics or the city's volunteer fire companies. Influential and wealthy Protestants in the city supported the committee as a means of dominating the Irish Catholic working class. One by one, targeted Irishmen were deported. The Vigilance Committee then made the mistake of targeting Tom Maguire, the local theater entrepreneur. Maguire, a longtime friend of Broderick's, was viewed as either a hardworking businessman or a well-connected scoundrel. Nonetheless, the vigilantes were challenged and backed off, rescinding the order against Maguire.

Governor J. Neely Johnson called on the local branch of the state militia to take back control of the city, but its major general, William Sherman, resigned when he realized the militia was outmanned and outgunned by the vigilantes. Sherman returned to his bank management job.

The committee next pursued Broderick himself, ordering his arrest and raising eyebrows throughout San Francisco. Just what were the vigilantes up to, and whom did they really represent? Their actions seemed to have more to do with party politics than crime. Were they front men for William Gwin and the local Chivs, or did they work for Henry Foote and the Know-Nothing Party? Neither Gwin nor Foote responded publicly. Broderick himself met with the committee to challenge its claims against him, negotiated a compromise and avoided arrest. With his political machine derailed and his loyal operatives run out, Broderick then quickly left town. But the committee wasn't done yet. It ultimately wanted political power more than criminal justice and was transformed into a political party: the People's Party. Dominated by local Protestant businessmen, the People's Party ruled San Francisco for more than a decade. It signified the businessmen's revolution against both the Chivalry and the Shovelry and threatened the state Democratic Party, particularly Broderick and Gwin. The People's Party would eventually be absorbed into the newly established Republican Party.

Sherman later noted that the members of the committee had controlled enough of the local press to write its own history, thereby favorably representing itself as the savior of the city.

The following April, in mutual agreement with his St. Louis–based employers, Sherman began the process of closing the San Francisco branch of the Bank of Lucas, Turner and Co. with plans to relocate to New York

City (the 1854 bank building is now characterized as Sherman's Bank). In May 1857, he and his family left the city.

While gold brought the world to the West, the silver rush that began in 1859 with an ore vein discovery in the western Utah territory[35] brought worldliness to San Francisco. This second rush poured millions of dollars into the city, transforming it from a rough-around-the-edges gold rush capital to a sophisticated silver metropolis. Silver actually generated approximately ten times the amount of wealth that gold had and created many local millionaires, including the big four Silver Kings—John MacKay, James Flood (Flood building/mansion), James Fair (Fairmont Hotel) and William O'Brien, whose offices were in the Montgomery Block—as well as George Hearst, the most successful miner of the era and the father of William Randolph Hearst, newspaper tycoon; Adolph Sutro, who later became mayor of San Francisco and built Sutro Baths and the second (seven-story, French chateau) Cliff House; William Ralston; and William Sharon. Ralston founded the Bank of California in 1864; Sharon was the bank's longtime Nevada agent. Ralston also built the first Palace Hotel and the California Theatre.

A San Francisco resident during the 1850s, William Tecumseh Sherman was a local banker before returning to the East Coast, destined to serve in the Union army. *Courtesy Library of Congress.*

The silver discovery, which also included substantial amounts of gold, completely overwhelmed San Francisco's mint, which had already outgrown its Commercial Street location. In 1874, the mint was relocated to a new granite-and-sandstone structure at Fifth and Mission Streets, a grand edifice that still stands and is now known as the Old Mint.

Chapter 9

Political Theater

Dissatisfaction with the timid positions of the Whig, Know-Nothing and Democratic Parties regarding slavery and its potential expansion to the West led to the formation of the Republican Party in 1854. The Republican Party became the principal opposition to the then-Southern-dominated Democratic Party. At its first national convention in June 1856, Republicans approved the antislavery platform, called for an end to polygamy and supported federal assistance for the transcontinental railroad. The new party nominated John C. Frémont, the former senator from California, as its first candidate in the presidential election of 1856. Frémont had the advantage of being nationally well known while not having much of a political track record. He could easily mimic the Republican platform while avoiding any mention of his low standing back in California. William Sherman, who had first met Frémont in 1847, commented that if Frémont qualified as a presidential candidate, then anyone did. William Dayton, a former senator from New Jersey, was chosen over Abraham Lincoln to fill the vice presidential slot.

As was common at the time, John Frémont was a reticent campaigner. Uncommon was his wife, Jessie's, active engagement with his campaign. As the daughter of Senator Benton and having grown up in the nation's capital, she understood Washington politics better than her husband did. Frémont's campaign slogan was "Free Speech, Free Soil, Free Men, Frémont"[36] and on to victory. Democratic candidate James Buchanan, meanwhile, warned potential voters that Republicans were extremists and that their winning the 1856 election would almost certainly lead to a civil war. A native Pennsylvanian, Buchanan had adopted a Southern perspective and believed that most slaves were well treated and that there was no reason to end the South's peculiar institution. He would take 174 electoral votes, while Frémont would manage to garner 114, winning almost 1.4 million of the popular vote versus Buchanan's 1.8. Not a bad showing for Frémont, who wasn't even on the ballot in most of the Southern states. Buchanan won all the slave states plus five of the free states, including California.

Despite losing, the Republican Party impressed many with its strong performance in the 1856 election. It was a party full of vigor and enthusiasm that had swelled to more than 1 million supporters, alarming Southerners and stoking animosities between the North and the South. Its beginnings coincided with that of the American feminist movement, which had grown out of the antislavery movement. The Republican Party was viewed as being the more progressive, and the Frémonts represented the model for an equal partnership between husbands and wives. Jessie Frémont's role during the 1856 election was far greater than most could have imaged, and Lincoln himself told her "that she was 'quite a female politician.'"[37] Democrats derisively suggested that Jessie was the real candidate and a vote for John

The "Pathfinder to the West" was unable to find the path that would successfully lead him to the White House in 1856. *Courtesy Library of Congress.*

Frémont was a vote for her, giving Jessie the opportunity to run the country and wreck the Union from behind the scenes. Though a loss, the Frémont candidacy had moved the party and the antislavery cause forward. By 1858, the Republican Party dominated the Northern states. Victories were ahead for the party, as was the secession that would follow.

Two days after Buchanan's inauguration, the U.S. Supreme Court handed down the Dred Scott decision. This 1857 decision by the Southern-dominated court stated that the Missouri Compromise was unconstitutional and confirmed that all federal territories would remain open to slavery. Southerners were delighted; Northerners were appalled. The crack in the national Democratic Party that had begun with the admission of California in 1850 widened as a result of the Dred Scott decision.

The Democratic Party had held its first meeting in San Francisco's Portsmouth Square within a month following the conclusion of the Constitutional Convention of 1849. *Alcalde* John Geary presided. The party would dominate California politics throughout the 1850s, with David Broderick and William Gwin fighting for control while representing different factions. As 1855 began, Gwin's first term as senator was almost at its end. He planned to run for reelection but became involved in a dispute regarding federal patronage, which led to a duel. Both parties missed, but this disagreement opened an opportunity for some maneuvering by Broderick, then chairman of the California Democratic Party, temporarily blocking a second term for Gwin. He successfully managed to impede Gwin's reelection until Senator John Weller's term also expired. By that point, it was time for a truce and a deal. Gwin and Broderick clandestinely met at the Magnolia Hotel in Sacramento. In exchange for Broderick's support for another term in the U.S. Senate, Gwin agreed to give Broderick control of all federal patronage in California. David Broderick then ran for the other U.S. Senate seat himself in 1856, succeeding Weller, while Gwin finally won reelection for his own Senate seat. Both were sworn in as senators in the first quarter of 1857 during the Buchanan administration. Neither had escaped attracting controversy over the years. Broderick's temperament and tactics had earned him a reputation as a bully, a self-serving opportunist and a danger to Southern interests. He was often aggressive and rude and called "Boss Broderick" behind his back. Gwin, who had represented the free state of California in Congress since 1850, had never relinquished ownership of his Mississippi plantation and the two hundred slaves on it. He had also maintained a tight grip on federal patronage in California. The truce was short-lived, and tensions between the two continued. It would all come to a head in 1859.

A Western Theater for Northern & Southern Politics

With Broderick now serving in Congress, the California state legislature nominated John Weller for governor. Weller won easily and would serve from 1858 to 1860. He planned to make California an independent republic if the North and South formally divided over the slavery issue. One result of Weller's victory was that the lion's share of state patronage would go to Southerners.

Returning to his city of birth, Senator Broderick found the nation's capital was much too Southern for his taste. He found it difficult to arrange a meeting with President Buchanan to discuss federal patronage issues. This wasn't what Broderick expected, particularly after having earnestly campaigned throughout California on behalf of Buchanan's election. When he finally met with Buchanan, the president held him at arm's length and wouldn't even address patronage. Unbeknownst to Broderick, he was being undercut by a barrage of letters from San Francisco Chivs, who were determined to destroy any influence that Broderick might wield in Washington and jeopardize the feasibility of any candidates he might put forth. To Broderick's dismay, the important position of port collector for San Francisco went to a Virginia native with the grand name of Benjamin Franklin Washington,[38] who was a former editor of a Chiv newspaper, the *San Francisco Times and Transcript*. Broderick realized that local Chivalry had been reinvigorated and was united against him.

As the youngest member of the Senate, Broderick responded to defenses of slavery made by Southern senators "in the language of 'Young America'":

> *Slavery is old, decrepit, and consumptive; freedom is young, strong and vigorous. The one is naturally stationary and loves ease; the other is migratory and enterprising...Wherever there is land for settlement,* [free workers] *will rush in and occupy it, and the compulsory labor of slaves will have to give way before the intelligent labor of free men.*[39]

Broderick pointed out to his colleagues that the columns of the Senate chamber itself were the work of his own father, a master stone carver. His gesture and his speech were not appreciated by his Southern senatorial colleagues. California Chivalry Democrats condemned Broderick for his insolent language.

A new movement to split the state in two resurfaced in 1859, and it came from the southern half via Andrés Pico, a state assemblyman who represented Los Angeles. The concern for Pico and the prominent Mexican families he represented was unfair taxation. Breaking away from

Northern California and becoming a territory, specifically the Territory of Colorado, was the proposed solution. Pico found plenty of backers in the Chiv-dominated state legislature for his proposal, but not because they cared about taxation as much as they cared about this latest opportunity to bring slavery to the southern half of California. The state legislature passed the Pico bill, and Governor Weller signed it. Broderick flew into action, traveling around the state making stump speeches and challenging Gwin to join him. Gwin eventually did so but generally found himself addressing hundreds, whereas Broderick would speak in front of thousands. The two more often spoke out against each other rather than addressing the issue at hand. Insults, innuendos and invectives flew back and forth. Nonetheless, the Pico bill was ratified and directed to Washington for congressional approval. Broderick was disappointed but not entirely surprised. He had lost ground in Sacramento and also in San Francisco, where his political power was in jeopardy.

Justice David Terry[40] of the California Supreme Court hated vigilante justice and stepped in to work with Governor Johnson to end its reign of terror. Terry himself became directly involved with the vigilantes when he stabbed one of them. Terry was held for seven weeks at Fort "Gunnybags," the Vigilance Committee's headquarters on Sacramento Street. Had this vigilante died, Terry would have likely gone to the gallows. Broderick used his influence, and charges against Terry were dropped. Nonetheless, Terry was repeatedly involved in violent acts during his residency in California, and three years later, he would become directly involved in the most memorable of San Francisco duels.

Dueling, the "Code of the West," proliferated in California. Gwin had failed to have duels outlawed, as per the 1849 constitution. In April 1850, San Francisco assemblyman George P. Johnston pushed through legislation that called for a prison sentence and payment of restitution by anyone convicted of dueling. The California state "legislature made dueling illegal in 1854, but juries refused to convict, and more duels were fought in California in the 1850s than in any other state of the Union."[41]

Duels were not only expressions of formalized political violence but also theatrical spectacles. They featured leading and supporting players and an audience of spectators gathered in anticipation of the upcoming performance. The Broderick-Terry deadly drama began at just about daybreak on the second Tuesday of September 1859.[42] Just about six dozen individuals gathered for a second time in as many days in a field within sight of the eastern shores of the *Laguna de la Merced*. They had

The August 16, 1856 edition of *Frank Leslie's Illustrated Newspaper* featured this image showing Justice Terry of the California Supreme Court stabbing Vigilance Committee member Sergeant Hopkins. *Courtesy San Francisco History Center, San Francisco Public Library.*

journeyed to an area that straddled the San Francisco/San Mateo County line to take part in or to witness the scene that would prove fatal to at least one man. The lead roles were assumed by Senator David Broderick and former chief justice David Terry, who had resigned his position in order to participate in the duel. A Southerner from Kentucky by way of Texas and a member of the elite planter class, Terry had arrived in California in 1849. He viewed the Free-Soilers, like Broderick, as "black Republicans" and "Negro lovers." Terry had stated in a speech that Senator Broderick took his cues from Frederick Douglass, a well-known black abolitionist. Broderick read Terry's comments in the newspaper, was incensed and responded in kind, declaring him to be "a damned miserable wretch." When Broderick publicly stated that both Terry and Gwin were corrupt, along with then-president Buchanan, Terry was outraged. He demanded satisfaction and challenged Broderick to a duel. Broderick accepted the challenge. It would not be his first, but it would be his last.

The parties in question had originally met on Monday the twelfth near the Davis milk farm[43] in San Mateo County, about one and a half miles south of the San Francisco County line, where they were promptly arrested by San Francisco chief of police Martin Burke.[44] The duelists were summoned to appear in front of Police Judge Henry Coon that same afternoon. Coon, who was destined to become mayor of San Francisco in 1863, reminded them that dueling had been outlawed. With no law having been violated (yet), they were discharged. After the hearing, the duel was surreptitiously rescheduled.

The next morning, the two principals, their seconds and a sizable group of observers again traveled through the outside lands of the city, reconvening behind the barn at the Lake House Ranch, east of Lake Merced.[45] The duelists each brought their own set of weapons and tossed to determine which set would be used. Terry won the toss, which put the outcome of the duel in his favor as he had practiced in advance with the "eight-inch Belgian pistols"[46] that, unbeknownst to Broderick, featured hair triggers.

The air was crisp as the rising sun attempted to break through the low-hanging fog, which gently and silently moved around the trees. Broderick and Terry were positioned back to back in the center of a clearing under the emerging blue skies. They then each walked forward the traditional ten paces, turned to face each other and simultaneously raised their respective pistols. Broderick accidentally fired first, hitting the ground. Terry, unharmed, aimed and shot Broderick point-blank in the chest. His intent, he said later, was to wound, not kill. Broderick, initially thought to be only superficially wounded, was transported to the Black Point home of his friend Leonidas Haskell. He died there on Friday morning, September 16, 1859.[47] He was thirty-nine.

During the last century and a half, several residents of the Haskell House have reported that it's seemingly haunted by a man wearing a long black coat and a top hat who would occasionally be sighted pacing about. Could this ghostly image be that of David Broderick?[48] Perhaps Broderick's spirit remains troubled because David Terry was never properly prosecuted for his role in the duel, which many at the time viewed as an outright assassination. Broderick's supporters felt that the Chivs were collectively responsible for Broderick's death. In their view, Terry merely served as the triggerman, eliminating Broderick from the political scene. As it turned out, Broderick's violent death would be a significant setback for the pro-Southern faction of the Democratic Party in California and a boost for the Free-Soilers, who made the most of it. The outcome of the duel significantly cleansed Broderick's image. Local public sentiment generally supported the late David Broderick and the antislavery cause.

The 1859 Broderick-Terry duel site. These granite shafts are positioned approximately where Senator David Broderick and former chief justice David Terry stood during the duel. *Courtesy of the author.*

Congress declared an official thirty-day mourning period in honor of Senator Broderick. His body lay in state at the Union Hotel across from Portsmouth Square, where he had lived for several years. Local public buildings, including firehouses, were draped in black crape; flags at city hall and throughout the city were at half-mast. Approximately thirty thousand people filled the square on Sunday the eighteenth for Broderick's funeral, during which he was eulogized by his good friend Edward D. Baker and an array of Free-Soil politicians as an antislavery martyr and the "Pacific Coast Lincoln." Baker declared to the thousands gathered for the funeral that Broderick's "death was a political necessity, poorly veiled beneath the guise of a private quarrel…What was his public crime? The answer is in his own words: 'I die because I was opposed to a corrupt administration and the extension of slavery.'"[49]

Following Broderick's funeral, California's remaining senator, William Gwin, left San Francisco to return to Washington. He found the nation's

A grand monument erected by the state of California marked the burial site for David Broderick in San Francisco's Laurel Hill Cemetery. Broderick's remains (but not the monument) were moved to Cypress Lawn Cemetery in 1942. *Courtesy Library of Congress.*

capital up in arms following the John Brown raid at Harpers Ferry and more bitterly divided than ever. Republicans had made impressive gains in recent state elections, unsettling Southerners. More than a few members of Congress now came to the capitol fully armed. The Pico bill had no chance at all in the prevailing environment and was deemed dead on arrival. California would remain fully intact as one state, a state that would continue to disallow slavery.

The split in the California Democratic Party opened opportunities for powerful capitalists who sought to influence California politics through their control of the mines, shipping and finance. They formed the California Republican Party and elected Leland Stanford (New York) as governor in 1861. Stanford had long despised slavery, and one of his priorities was keeping California in the Union during the Civil War years. While Stanford proved to be a capable governor, he was not re-nominated for another term in 1863. He had been undone by statewide Democratic political machinations and chose instead to concentrate on other issues, such as bringing the railroad to the West. Stanford would be succeeded by another Republican, Frederick Low.

Chapter 10

San Francisco Players

John and Jessie Frémont returned to San Francisco in 1858. Despite Frémont's defeat in the 1856 presidential election, he and Jessie remained a socially and politically well-connected couple. By 1860, they and their children had settled into their new home—a Black Point cottage located at Point San José in the city's northern district. The name "Black Point" came from the dense carpet of black mountain laurel greenery in the vicinity, and their home was among five houses (including the Haskell House) in the immediate area. The combination of Jessie's hospitality, the gardens and the expansive views attracted a steady stream of visitors. Mrs. Frémont delighted in her life back in San Francisco, and she enjoyed opera from her private box at Maguire's Opera House, along with dramas at the city's many theaters. Jessie also enjoyed hearing a variety of lecturers, and one day in late April 1860, she heard the Reverend Thomas Starr King speak at his First Unitarian Church. Jessie was captivated by his oratory and quickly became very supportive of the Reverend King. King was a New York native who had come west after many years in Massachusetts. The Frémonts invited the Reverend and Mrs. King to dinner within a month of their arrival in San Francisco. They stood by as King christened their new home, viewing him as a potentially valuable ally in their continued fight against slavery.

The Frémonts brought the Kings up to date by reviewing the local events of the 1850s. They regarded Reverend King's oratorical skills and pulpit as tremendous assets and impressed upon him the need to use them to speak out against slavery. King agreed to do so, and Jessie Frémont, a

A Western Theater for Northern & Southern Politics

Jessie Benton Frémont at her Black Point cottage, which became a political and literary salon for writers, artists and politicians, not to mention radicals, misfits and loners. *Courtesy San Francisco History Center, San Francisco Public Library.*

lapsed Episcopalian, was so impressed with King's eloquence and upbeat personality that she purchased a pew in his Unitarian church.

When Thomas Starr King and his wife first arrived in San Francisco, the First Unitarian Church that he was to lead was then located just up the hill from Portsmouth Square. It was there that the Reverend King enthusiastically threw himself into the role of both leading the Unitarian congregation and defending the interests of the Northern states. He reminded his congregation, particularly those who were members of the Southern Chivalry, that "the North has frequently had to tolerate a Southerner or pro-South man as president, and yet has stayed in the Union."[50] While tacitly acknowledging that point, local Southerners were dismayed by the stir King's preaching

Reverend Thomas Starr King was credited by President Lincoln for his efforts in keeping California in the Union. *Courtesy Library of Congress.*

caused, particularly as he also regularly reminded his congregation of the martyred David Broderick. They began to stay away from his church. Within a month of his arrival in San Francisco, in a letter to a friend in New York, King noted that "the Southerners out here are down on me because, they say, I am a strong anti-slavery man. They refuse to patronize my lectures on that ground, and said that I must not be countenanced."[51]

The Frémonts were also friends with Edward Baker. Baker had practiced law in Illinois, where he became a close friend of Abraham Lincoln, so much so that Lincoln named his second son for him. Baker twice served in the House of Representatives for Illinois districts. His law and legislative careers were interrupted by military service in the Mexican-American War. Following the war, in 1852, Baker and his family moved to San Francisco, where he became known for both his legal and oratorical skills. His law office was located just across from the bank that Sherman managed. Baker became good friends with David Broderick, who spent the Sunday night before the Broderick-Terry duel as a guest at Baker's home. Baker's funeral oration at Broderick's service was so stirring that it would be printed as a pamphlet. Its circulation around the state served to further rally Free-Soil opinion against Southern slave interests.

Colonel Baker had traveled tirelessly throughout California in 1856 speaking on behalf of the Frémont/Dayton Republican national ticket. His speaking style, combined with his magnetic personality, drew in listeners, particularly in the smaller towns. Baker's efforts went a long way toward spreading information about the Republican Party and its platform. They did not win the state for Frémont/Dayton, however, and California's four electoral votes went to Buchanan; San Francisco voters only marginally supported the Frémont/Dayton ticket. Nonetheless, Baker's efforts were not in vain, and he became known as the Silver Eagle of republicanism. Eleven days before the November 1860 election, he eloquently addressed a packed house at the American Theatre that included the Frémonts and the Kings. Baker spoke out against the evils of slavery and in favor of Lincoln's candidacy and the Free-Soilers and referenced the death of Broderick, which had occurred a year earlier. His moving talk enthralled the audience and included this passage:

> *We are running a man now by the name of Lincoln* [cheers from the audience]...*He is an honest, good, simple-minded, true man who is a hero without knowing it...but his hands must be upheld and strengthened by you. You must send men to Congress who will not feel that the "peculiar institution"* [of slavery] *is the only institution there is.*[52]

Baker's more than two-hour oration on that October day would become known as the "Apostrophe to Freedom" speech. It, too, would be printed in pamphlet form. The speech would be posted on bulletin boards and read aloud to assembled groups throughout the state in the days leading up to the November 1860 presidential election.

Baker's speech further split the Democratic Party in California and Oregon. Both states were carried by Lincoln and the Republicans. Lincoln, however, just barely won California with 32.3 percent of the vote. Stephen A. Douglas, the Northern Democratic candidate, was a close second with 31.7 percent, while the Southern Democratic candidate, John C. Breckinridge, who was backed by Gwin, won 28.4 percent (John Bell, the candidate for the Constitutional Union party, formed by Southern Unionists, won the remaining 7.6 percent). Statewide, only 614 votes separated Lincoln and Douglas. It's telling that "[i]n no other free state did so large a proportion of voters cast ballots against the Republican candidate."[53] Lincoln did win a plurality in San Francisco County and

San Francisco attorney Edward Baker avidly campaigned on behalf of the Republican Party and for his friend Abraham Lincoln. Baker was then chosen to introduce Lincoln at his 1861 presidential inaugural in Washington, D.C. *Courtesy Library of Congress.*

eight other California counties, thus winning the state's four electoral votes.⁵⁴ San Francisco voters backed Lincoln by almost 48.0 percent; 28.0 percent supported Douglas and 18.0 percent, Breckinridge.⁵⁵ Lingering anger over the death of Broderick significantly contributed to Lincoln's victory in the city. While the combination of votes for Lincoln and Douglas equaled 76.0 percent, a clear antislavery majority, "[h]ad Lincoln not obtained a plurality of 2,790 votes in San Francisco, he would not have won the California election."⁵⁶ While "lightning messages" announced Lincoln's 1860 election to the North and the South, it was the Pony Express that brought the news to San Francisco and the West.

Defeated in his bid for a California congressional seat in 1859 (a loss engineered by Gwin), Edward Baker was elected a senator in 1860 from the new state of Oregon.

In his memoirs published in 1875, General William Tecumseh Sherman recalled, "The election of Mr. Lincoln fell upon us all like a clap of thunder. People saw and felt that the South had threatened so long that, if she quietly submitted, the question of slavery in the Territories was at an end forever."⁵⁷

As with so many antebellum households, the Booth brothers were divided in their loyalties. Edwin and June were both Unionists and in favor of Lincoln's 1860 election. John Wilkes was a committed supporter of the South and a staunch secessionist. He frequently spoke out against Lincoln and the North. When he did this in Northern cities, residents often told him to shut up or get out of town. In general, Edwin theatrically dominated in the North, John in the South and June in the West.

While Jessie Frémont largely supported Lincoln's election, she couldn't help but realize that if the Democratic Party had not split prior to the 1856 election, her own husband would likely have been elected president. John Frémont had moved on to other endeavors. He left San Francisco on January 1, 1861, for a trip to the East and Europe, accompanied by his attorney, Frederick Billings of Halleck, Peachy and Billings. On that same January day, San Francisco newspapers reported that South Carolina had withdrawn from the Union. The Great Secession Winter of 1860–61 had begun, as Northern Democrats and Southern Unionists, positioned in between Republican abolitionists and Southern secessionists, had been unable to prevent the inevitability of the long-simmering Southern secession. The changing political landscape and the certainty of war were unsettling for Jessie, and in a letter to Thomas Starr King, she noted: "The fear of what may be in store for us all if this cloud of civil war takes shape, makes me restless."⁵⁸

A Western Theater for Northern & Southern Politics

The Reverend King was himself alarmed by the secession of Southern states and by the possibility that California itself might be maneuvered into joining the developing Confederacy. That threat ignited his fiery campaign to keep California in the Union and to speak out on behalf of the Lincoln presidency. He began with a speech to a packed house at Tucker's Academy of Music in San Francisco on Washington's Birthday, 1861. The enthusiastic crowd, which included Jessie Frémont, clapped and cheered King's impassioned oration.

A few blocks away stood the Calvary Presbyterian Church. At its pulpit was Dr. William A. Scott, a New Orleans native, who interlaced his sermons with talk of disunion and preached in support of Southern views on national issues, including slavery. Members of Scott's congregation were not entirely surprised to arrive at his church one Sunday morning to find a likeness of the pastor hanged in effigy near the front entrance. Undaunted, Dr. Scott continued preaching against Lincoln's election and the North. Upon the

Dr. William Scott's Calvary Presbyterian Church on Bush Street was established in 1854. It had a Roman-temple façade and was located between Platt's Hall and the Mercantile Library. This view looks east toward Sansome Street. *Courtesy Calvary Presbyterian Church Archives.*

establishment of the Confederate States of America, he offered public prayers on behalf of CSA president Jefferson Davis. After being hanged in effigy for a second time, Dr. Scott decided to leave San Francisco.

Realizing that his congregation had outgrown its church building, the Reverend King supervised the construction of a new church five blocks farther south. It was financed by parishioners' loans along with funds generated by King through a local lecture series. The new church building on Geary Street was dedicated in January 1864.

In addition to preaching inside his new church, the Reverend King also regularly spoke at a public park across the street then surrounded by Victorian homes and other houses of worship. The 2.6 acres of land for this park had been donated to the city in 1850 by its first American mayor, John Geary. Reverend King tirelessly made speeches and led rallies at this park supporting Lincoln and the North. The largest of these would occur on May 11, 1861, following the firing on Fort Sumter, ultimately attracting twenty-five thousand people. Pro-Union patriotism surfaced as they marched through the city's streets. Placards were posted and banners held high, displaying quotes from the late Secretary of State Daniel Webster. These included "THE UNION, THE WHOLE UNION & NOTHING BUT THE UNION" and "LIBERTY and UNION, now and forever, ONE AND INSEPARABLE." Webster, a New Englander, had, along with Henry Clay, been a strong advocate for the preservation of the Union. This rally and San Francisco's support for the North prompted the park across from King's church to become known as Union Square.

Reverend King also organized the Pacific branch of the predecessor of the American Red Cross, the U.S. Sanitary Commission. His efforts raised $1.5 million for the organization, which represented more than a quarter of the total raised nationwide and went a long way for the benefit of sick and wounded soldiers. King periodically embarked on lecture tours through the state's interior counties defending the Union's interests, generally facing gun- and knife-toting audiences while carrying no weapon of his own. As he well knew, a good portion of these audiences was composed of Southern sympathizers. The danger was palpable, to be sure, but exhilarating at the same time. King visited mining camps and towns full of crusty, old miners with strong opinions. Despite the circumstances, King's speeches were often poetic and eloquent, perhaps in an effort to placate his audiences.

In June 1860, President Buchanan had signed the Pacific Telegraph Act, which allocated funds for the continuation of the telegraph line westward from Missouri to Sacramento and San Francisco. This transcontinental

Banners quoting Daniel Webster were featured at this pro-Union rally at Market, Post and Montgomery Streets on May 11, 1861. The Aetna/McKesson Building has occupied the One Post Street site since 1969. *Courtesy San Francisco History Center, San Francisco Public Library.*

telegraph line was completed by October 1861. One of the first West-to-East messages to be telegraphed, originating in San Francisco, was from the Reverend King. In it, he noted that the telegraph represented "a new band of Union between the Pacific and the Atlantic. The lightning now goeth out of the West and speaks even to the East. Heaven preserve the Republic."[59]

Jessie Frémont received a letter from her husband in May 1861 advising that he had been named major general by President Lincoln. He was put in charge of the Department of the West, which encompassed the region from the Mississippi River to the Rocky Mountains. Jessie rented out her Black Point home and its furnishings to Edward Beale. She and her five children sailed out of San Francisco on June 21 to meet John in the bitterly divided city of St. Louis. Joining them was their Black Point neighbor Leonidas Haskell, who would serve as General Frémont's chief of staff.

Chapter 11

The Shadow of War in San Francisco

As the *Tennessee* and the *California* sailed through Golden Gate Straits, passengers, such as the Hitchcocks and the Booths, might have noticed the remains of the old *Castillo de San Joaquin*. This fort had been established in the late eighteenth century during the Spanish era in Alta California as part of its *presidio* (military outpost). The Spaniards had named the site *Punta del Cantil Blanco* (White Cliff Point). The *castillo* was abandoned during the Mexican era. When the Americans arrived in the late 1840s, they renamed the old *castillo* Fort Blanco and the area it occupied Fort Point. The incredible wealth flowing from the gold fields, combined with simmering tensions related to the slavery issue, motivated the U.S. Army to shore up defenses near the Golden Gate. It began by installing artillery pieces in the remains of the old *castillo*. This was a temporary remedy until 1852, when the old *castillo* and the bluff behind it were demolished, creating a level platform for the construction of the new American fort. Granite for its foundation was imported from China, while the bricks for the walls would be made at a brickyard just south of the site. The building of the fort began in 1853, with much of the work done by unemployed miners. Reports of the shot fired at Fort Sumter in April 1861 hastened its completion. Fort Point, a scaled-down version of Fort Sumter,[60] then stood at the ready for potential attacks by sea.

Located just three miles inside the Golden Gate, the lonely island of Alcatraz was first viewed as a potential American military site during the Mexican-American War era. "Alcatraz Island suggest[ed] the appearance

Fort Point at Golden Gate Straits, looking north toward Marin County. Today, the Golden Gate Bridge spans the straits, extending over a portion of the fort. *Courtesy San Francisco History Center, San Francisco Public Library.*

of a battleship permanently anchored in defense of the Bay."[61] In 1846, John Frémont, acting in the capacity of American military governor of California, bought the island for $5,000 on behalf of the federal government. In November 1850, just two months after California became the thirty-first state, President Fillmore issued an executive order stating that Alcatraz and nearby Angel Island be set aside as military reservations. Sandstone from the quarry at Angel Island was used to construct the fortifications on Alcatraz (and at Fort Point). The first fully operational lighthouse on the West Coast was placed on Alcatraz Island in 1854. Fort Alcatraz was fully fortified by

1858 and at the start of the Civil War featured ninety-one cannons, eight officers and approximately 361 soldiers; the island was the most heavily fortified site on the West Coast. Alcatraz housed civilian and military prisoners, along with menacing Confederate sympathizers and Southern privateers then operating on the West Coast. The number of prisoners on the island at any given time fluctuated and numbered about four dozen by the end of the war in 1865.

Nearby Angel Island had been a popular site for duels for over a decade by the time formal fortifications on the island began. In 1863, batteries and buildings for a military post were constructed. The camp was given the name of Camp Reynolds in honor of Major General John F. Reynolds, who had died a hero at the Battle of Gettysburg. The camp would eventually include officers' quarters, enlisted men's barracks and a chapel. Soldiers from the fort on Alcatraz had, as early as the 1860s,

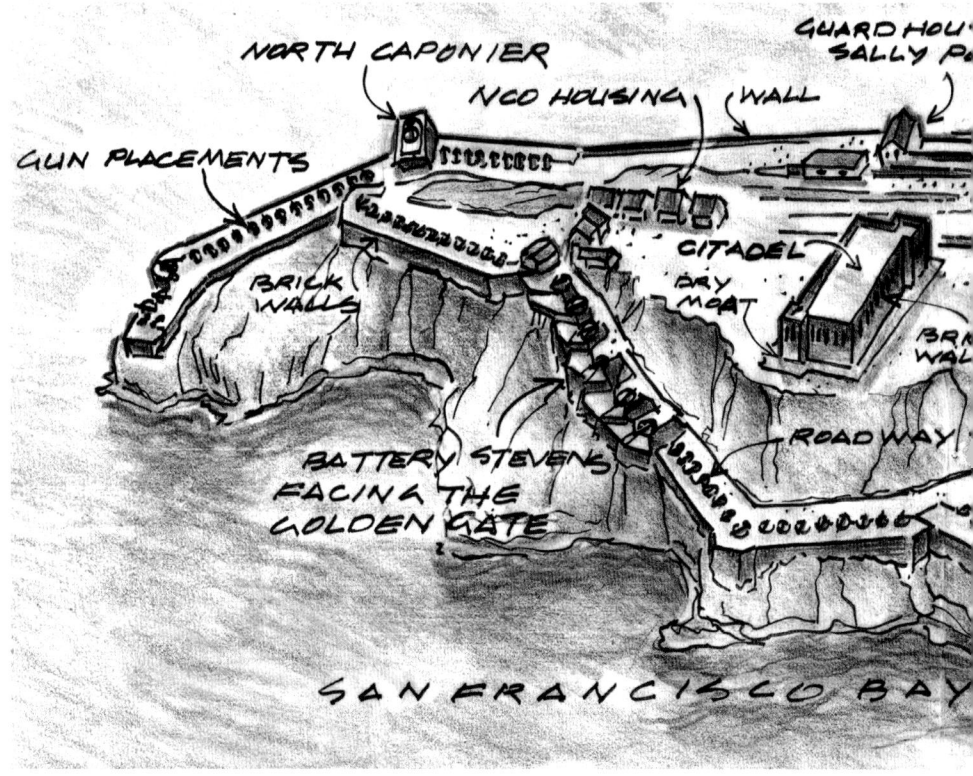

During the war, Alcatraz Island served as a prison for local Confederate sympathizers and Southern privateers deemed guilty of disloyalty to the Union; some of them referred to Fort Alcatraz as Fort Union. *Courtesy of Donald MacDonald.*

designated that island as a "rock" and came to Angel Island to establish vegetable gardens. The former location of these gardens on the south side of Angel Island is still referred to as "Alcatraz Gardens." Alcatraz and Angel Islands, strategically located just east of the Golden Gate, along with Fort Point to the south and Lime Point (eventually Fort Baker) on the north end of the Golden Gate, would form a triangular crossfire defense against any hostile ship that might enter into San Francisco Bay. Additional cannon batteries would be placed on Yerba Buena Island and along the shoreline at what is now Fort Mason. Thus was the defense against potential Confederate raiders. Ironically, detailed plans for the construction of the forts and batteries within San Francisco Bay were reviewed and approved by Jefferson Davis in 1852. At the time, Davis was U.S. secretary of war. A decade later, he would be president of the Confederate States of America.

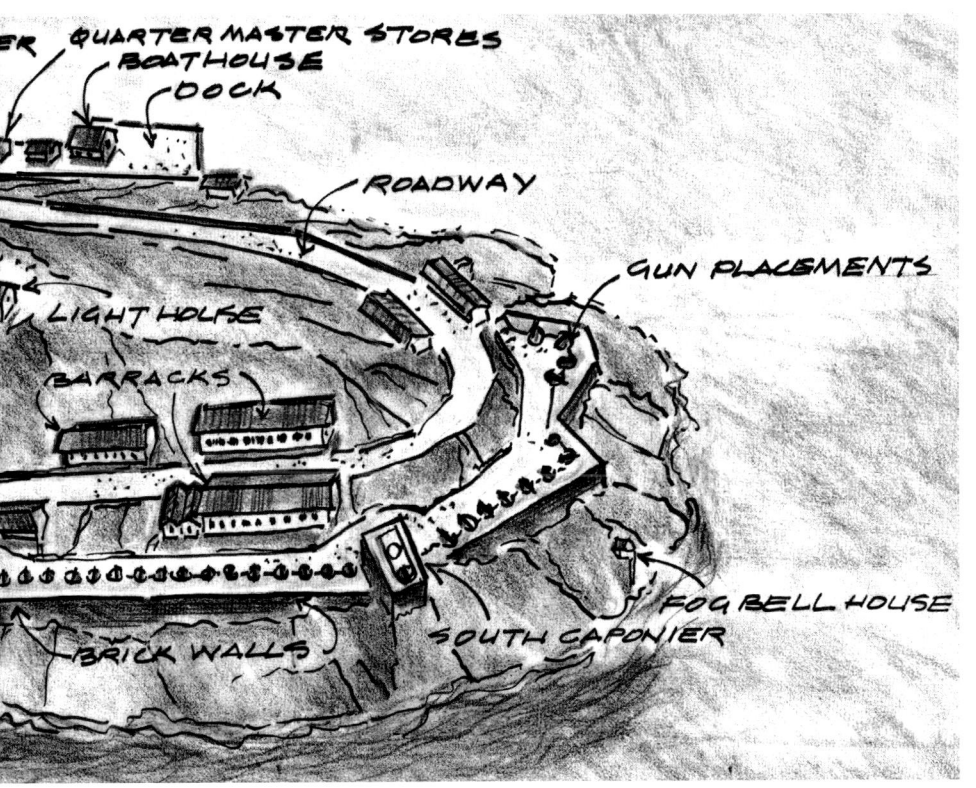

Antebellum and Civil War San Francisco

When Southern states began seceding from the Union, California secessionists supported the rebellion. Many of them formed the San Francisco chapter of a secret national organization named the Knights of the Golden Circle (KGC),[62] which was to provide local assistance to the Confederacy and had a rumored membership of sixteen thousand. Reputedly headed by Senator William Gwin, the KGC also had a secret pledge and a constitution, along with secret passwords used by its members. This organization and its Third Degree Knights of the Columbian Star plotted to take control of San Francisco and the Bay Area in order to divert gold shipments destined for the North to the Confederacy via Texas, thus significantly impeding the Union war effort. The conspirators hoped to recruit General Albert Sidney Johnston, commander of the Department of the Pacific,[63] to assist. While he had grown up in Texas, Johnston remained loyal to the U.S. Army and dismissed what he characterized as a foolish plot. Nonetheless, the KGC was well organized and intended to seize the Presidio, the mint, the customhouse, Fort Point, the arsenal at Benicia, the fortress at Alcatraz and other Federal properties once the war began. The state government in Sacramento was also to be seized. The scheme fell apart when a Union general, Edwin Sumner, arrived in San Francisco just days before the reports of the fall of Fort Sumter officially became known throughout the city. That news would arrive via the Pony Express on April 24. Sumner took firm control of the Bay Area's Federal properties for the Union from General Johnston. Johnston resigned from the army and headed down to Los Angeles. In June, he traveled east. General Johnston, who would later command the western army of the Confederacy, would be killed during the bloody battle at Shiloh in the spring of 1862. He was the highest-ranking officer, Confederate or Union, to die during the war.

General Sumner treaded carefully, not wanting to inflame West Coast secessionists. Despite their smaller numbers, he realized they were far more active and zealous—and thus more influential—than the Unionists. Sumner quietly removed potentially disloyal officers and employees from army posts and also terminated agreements with pro-Southern suppliers. He encouraged the organization of Unionist home guards and strengthened defenses up and down the Pacific coast, particularly in and around San Francisco. His goal was to keep the secessionists from becoming a serious threat.

By the time Lincoln was inaugurated in March 1861, seven states had already seceded. The Confederacy had been established in February and elected Dr. Hitchcock's old friend Jefferson Davis as its president. Four additional states would ultimately join the Confederacy. San Francisco became a fractured city that ostensibly supported the Union but had a sizable

A Western Theater for Northern & Southern Politics

Lillie Hitchcock (Coit) with her father, Dr. Charles Hitchcock, in San Francisco, circa 1861.
Courtesy San Francisco History Center, San Francisco Public Library.

residency with ties to the Confederate states. The idea of creating a completely independent republic was floated about. This plan called for California to join with the new state of Oregon and the western territories to form the Pacific Republic.[64] California's congressional representatives, led by Senator Gwin, were greatly in favor of establishing such a republic, whose eastern border would be the Rocky Mountains. They were also in favor of an eventual alliance with the Southern Confederacy. Meetings were held in San Francisco to discourage the idea, and the *Daily Alta California* printed articles and editorials against it.

The movement for the Pacific Republic largely dissipated when reports of the fall of Fort Sumter arrived in San Francisco. This information was hastily written on chalkboards that hung outside of local newspaper offices while the next editions were being prepared. This startling news sparked overwhelming local support for the Union. Flags were raised throughout the city, speeches were given supportive of Lincoln and the Union cause and Confederate president Jefferson Davis was hanged in effigy. Local Southerners grew silent, afraid of being branded as traitors and unsure of how to proceed. Dr. Hitchcock received a separate message via the Pony Express: President Davis offered him the post of medical director of the Confederate army. However, the Maryland native strongly felt that the agriculturally based South had no chance of winning against the industrialized North. In addition, he viewed himself more a West Point man than a Southerner and so declined Davis's offer.

The youngest Booth brother, Joseph, joined the Rebels in the attack on Fort Sumter. He had trained as a physician and would briefly serve with the Confederate army. But Joseph was not particularly interested in war (or acting) and left on a worldwide tour. Eventually, he made his way to San Francisco and his brother June's home on Telegraph Hill.

Once the war started, many military men who had gravitated to San Francisco in the 1840s and '50s began heading east to offer their services to the Union or Confederate army. By December 1861, approximately 313 officers from western states and territories left to fight for the North or the South. Conscription was not applied to states and territories west of the Rocky Mountains, so hundreds of ordinary men decided for themselves to travel back to their native states to enlist, financing their own transport. Approximately 16,000 California men volunteered to fight for the Union cause. California Unionists fought as part of the Second Massachusetts Cavalry and the Seventy-first Pennsylvania Volunteers. California volunteers were recruited by the Federal government to guard the overland mails and to secure the West from the Confederacy, occupying strategic points from the Puget Sound (Washington State) to the New Mexico Territory.

A Western Theater for Northern & Southern Politics

In 1861, 2,350 officers and men formed the "California Column." These Union volunteers consisted of infantry and cavalry soldiers and included Companies H and K from San Francisco. They were sent to the Los Angeles area to cope with the concentration of secessionists there and to guard against Texas forces, already in the New Mexico Territory, from potentially continuing on toward California. Following two skirmishes in 1862 (in Arizona), the California Column followed the retreating Confederates into West Texas. The column advanced two hundred miles into Texas, raising the American flag over Fort Quitman and preventing a resurgence of Confederates to the West.

The families of well-off, ardent Southerners, especially those who had joined the Confederate army, were generally sent out of the country. Mrs. Hitchcock and her daughter, Lillie, were among them and spent much of the war years attending concerts and socializing in England and amid the French court of Emperor Napoleon III.

The law firm of Halleck, Peachy and Billings flourished until the outbreak of the war. In 1861, the law firm was ostensibly dissolved when Archibald Peachy declared Halleck's support of the Northern cause to be unacceptable. Halleck left the firm to become a Union army general. He would later serve as President Lincoln's army chief of staff and would be the overall administrator of the Union army.

Various high-level military transients who spent time in California between the wars were called to service. Most of these men had previously served in the Mexican-American War. During the Civil War, William Tecumseh Sherman rose to the rank of Union army major general, and John C. Frémont was named commander of the Western Department. Ulysses S. Grant, who had intermittently lived in San Francisco in the early 1850s, succeeded Halleck as Lincoln's general-in-chief. Former mayor John Geary also served as a general for the Union

During the Civil War, Henry Halleck served as Lincoln's general-in-chief and, later, as one of his pallbearers. *Courtesy Library of Congress.*

army. In addition to Albert S. Johnston, James Longstreet and George Pickett (later to lead Pickett's Charge at Gettysburg) left California to serve the Confederacy as generals. Former California chief justice David Terry, the man who had shot David Broderick in 1859, served in the Eighth Texas Cavalry of the Confederate army. Many in San Francisco viewed Terry's shot as the first West Coast shot of the Civil War.

Edward Baker was appointed to lead a Union army regiment. Almost exactly a year after his American Theatre speech, he was killed in October 1861 during the Battle of Ball's Bluff (Virginia), a Confederate victory. The second telegram to arrive in San Francisco on the recently completed transcontinental telegraph line announced the news of Baker's death. Following funeral services in Washington, Colonel Baker's body was returned to San Francisco, where he was eulogized by his friend Reverend Thomas Starr King. Colonel Baker was then buried at the city's Lone Mountain Cemetery.[65]

The telegraph strengthened economic ties between the East and the West, particularly with respect to banking and investment houses. It put the Pony Express out of business and kept San Franciscans more acutely in

President Lincoln openly wept when he heard the news of the death of his old friend Edward Baker in October 1861. *Courtesy Library of Congress.*

touch with political- and war-related events. It also reminded Californians of the value of staying with the Union. Support for a separate Pacific Republic faded away. President Lincoln became the first national leader to make apt use of the telegraph to project his leadership, particularly with respect to military matters, through the transmissions of almost one thousand telegrams throughout his presidency. Simply stated, "[T]he telegraph was the e-mail of the 1800s and its impact back then was even more profound than today's 'information revolution.'"[66]

The war had only a minor effect on San Francisco's theatricals. Beginning in October 1861, news about the war was regularly telegraphed to the city. With the latest dispatches in hand, theater managers would announce the latest war-related news from their stages prior to performances. Theater owners responded to reports about the war's progress by occasionally sponsoring benefit performances to support victims of the war. Only a few war-oriented plays were performed in the city during the war years. For the most part, the usual array of theatrical performances was held in San Francisco theaters during those years. An important theatrical event in 1864 was the tercentennial of Shakespeare's birth. San Francisco theaters offered special programs in honor of Shakespeare's 300th birthday.

A local issue that vexed theater owners and managers was the stringent Blue Laws that the city passed in 1864 forcing theaters (and gambling houses) to close on Sundays. Blue Laws dated back to the 1850s but had never been particularly enforced. Tom Maguire, by then the owner of several theaters in the city, challenged the new 1864 version of these laws as he had lesser potent versions. The case worked its way up to the California State Supreme Court, but in the end, Maguire lost. Blue Laws would remain on the books until repealed by the California legislature in 1870.

Hoarding of gold and silver coins by the public had already begun in the late 1850s, increasing once the war began. When the Confederacy closed the branch mints in the southeastern states, it dramatically decreased the amount of coinage in practical usage. Only the San Francisco Mint continued full production during the war years. The Philadelphia Mint chose to store its coins, and in February 1862, Congress passed the Legal Tender Act, issuing $450 million in "greenbacks" to meet currency demands. By the summer of 1862, it was difficult to find gold or silver coinage in the Northern or Southern states. Greenbacks were not backed by gold and were fiat money. They were not welcomed in California, and San Francisco merchants rarely honored them. During

1864, $16,323,186 in gold and silver coins was minted in San Francisco. Coins produced in San Francisco would literally be worn out, as they were generally the only ones circulating in the first half of the 1860s.

Financing the war effort was, from the start, a challenging task for the Lincoln administration, which looked to the West's mineral resources to meet that challenge. Ships that sailed out of San Francisco Bay carried not only potential soldiers but also considerable amounts of gold from the mines of California and Nevada. Several times a month, a steamer ship would leave San Francisco carrying $1 million to $3 million in gold bound for the northeastern ports "to help arm, feed and clothe one million Union fighting men."[67] More than $100 million of gold would travel east during the war years. These shipments served to build up reserves at eastern banks, buying time for the U.S. Treasury Department, which looked for ways of meeting ongoing war-related expenses.

In July 1862, President Lincoln signed the Pacific Railway Act, which provided Federal support for the building of the long-awaited transcontinental railroad. This act had easily passed through Congress because Southern legislators, who likely would have voted to block it due to ongoing disagreements over its routing, weren't present to do so. One Southerner, California senator Gwin, had advocated for the railroad as early as 1851, believing its completion would give Californians a sense of truly being connected to the rest of the country. He echoed calls for a railroad that had already begun as soon as gold had been discovered. A transcontinental railroad was viewed as the solution for easier journeys to California and for easier transport of gold to the East, but congressional bickering had delayed the project again and again. Lincoln viewed the railroad's expansion to the West as an important unifier but would not live long enough to see its completion; it wouldn't be completed until four years after his death.

A grand fête took place at Platt's Hall in January 1863 during which San Francisco's approximately 1,200 black residents celebrated the announcement of President Lincoln's Emancipation Proclamation. While unable to vote, local blacks endorsed Lincoln for reelection in the upcoming 1864 election, having supported the Union throughout the antebellum and Civil War years. Their best hope for the future lay with Republican victories at the polls. It would be during Republican control of the state that the barriers of discrimination against blacks in California and segregation itself would begin to break down.

In October 1863, the Federal government commandeered the area known as Point San José, which included Black Point, for the establishment of a battery and troops. The Frémont home and property were confiscated, as were Leonidas Haskell's and several others. The military possession of the properties was carried out by Colonel Richard B. Mason, who had served as military governor of California in the 1840s and had had some acrimonious encounters with John Frémont during those years.[68] Under Mason's direction, the Frémont home was leveled. Jessie Frémont filed for restitution and compensation, to no avail. Eventually, the entire area would be renamed Fort Mason.

Years of work and travel finally caught up with Reverend King. Exhausted by his activities up and down the state speaking on behalf of the Lincoln and the Union, he died of diphtheria complicated by pneumonia in March 1864, just about a year before the war ended. He was thirty-nine. The city, shocked by his untimely death, once again went into mourning. Flags were

Reverend King's First Unitarian Church at Geary and Stockton Streets, circa 1864. King was interred on the grounds; his sarcophagus can be seen on the left. *Collection Society of California Pioneers, Lawrence & Houseworth Albums.*

lowered, public buildings were closed and the state legislature adjourned for three days. His body lay in state at his two-month-old church on Geary Street, where a continuous flow of mourners, including California governor Frederick Low, slowly moved past his casket. King would be buried on the grounds of his church.[69] The Reverend King's death, along with that of Edward Baker and David Broderick, united the three as casualties in the ongoing battle against slavery coming into California.[70]

In March 1863, the schooner *J.M. Chapman* was seized in the San Francisco harbor by the U.S. Navy. The *Chapman* had been secretly outfitted to operate as a Confederate raider along the West Coast to hijack gold and silver for the Confederacy. Once the war began, the South had been cut off from receiving any gold from California. It instead went to the New York banks or the U.S. Treasury in Washington. The leading conspirators in the plot, which included Asbury Harpending (Kentucky), were captured, and the *Chapman* was towed to Alcatraz.

One of Harpending's co-conspirators in the *Chapman* incident was an Englishman named Alfred Rubery, whose uncle John Bright was a member of Parliament. In 1863, Bright defeated a resolution in the House of Commons for an alliance between Britain, France and the Confederate states against the North. An outspoken critic of slavery and an admirer of Lincoln, Bright refused to use Southern cotton at his mills. He later appealed to the Lincoln administration on behalf of his nephew, who, along with the other *Chapman* plotters, had been tried for treason and received ten years' imprisonment at Fort Alcatraz plus a $10,000 fine. In January 1864, the president granted a pardon for Rubery with the stipulation that he leave the country within thirty days. Bright's testimonial in support of Lincoln's 1864 reelection would be found in Lincoln's pocket following his assassination. (In the 2012 film *Lincoln*, a photograph of Bright is displayed on the mantel in Lincoln's study, just as it was in 1865.)

San Francisco was particularly wary of a potential attack by the Confederate steam sloop CSS *Alabama*, and there was genuine fear that it would sneak into the bay under the cover of darkness and fog. In response to these concerns, an ironclad ship, the USS *Comanche*, was specially built to defend San Francisco Bay. Constructed in New Jersey, the *Comanche* was disassembled and loaded onto a wooden cargo ship, the *Aquila*, which then brought the pieces around the horn. The *Aquila* was greeted with much enthusiasm by the city's residents when it arrived on November 10, 1863, docking at a pier just east of Third Street (near today's AT&T Park). While waiting to be unloaded, the *Aquila* was subjected to a hurricane-

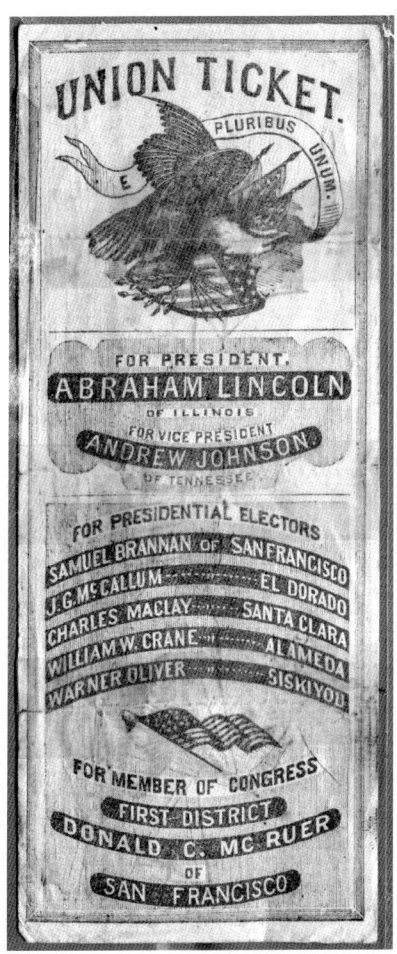

This 1864 Union ballot was used in San Francisco and listed Sam Brannan as a presidential elector. The California Republican Convention for that year's election was held at Platt's Hall at Montgomery and Bush Streets. *Courtesy of Robert J. Chandler.*

force windstorm that blew in on the night of November 14. The ship simply couldn't withstand the power of the winds and the waves during that overnight storm, and dawn revealed that the *Aquila* and its cargo of the *Comanche* had sunk. Debates began immediately among the citizenry. Was it truly a natural calamity, or was it, as some speculated, sabotage by local secessionists? Should it be raised? It would take a full year, but the *Comanche* was finally salvaged, reassembled and then launched in front of cheering crowds and playing bands. The ironclad ship was then ready in case of attack. None occurred. Five months later, the war ended.[71]

By 1864, political dynamics had changed in California, as they had nationally. Lincoln won the state in that year's election by a significant margin of 59.2 percent. For the second time, California's electoral votes, now numbering five, went to Lincoln, as did 58.0 percent of the San Francisco vote. The reunited Democratic Party put forth a single candidate in 1864: former Union army general George McClellan. McClellan had been commanding general of the Army of the Potomac until Lincoln fired him. Nationwide, President Lincoln won reelection with a comfortable margin of 55.0 percent. No popular or electoral votes were counted from the eleven states that comprised the Confederacy. The president's second inaugural address, given on March 4, 1865, in front of the U.S. Capitol, was the first such event to be photographed. Standing in the sizable crowd that surrounded Lincoln at the podium can be seen the image of John Wilkes Booth.

Chapter 12

The Curtain Falls

After thirteen years in San Francisco, June Booth and his family returned to New York in the spring of 1864. They reunited with the Booth family, including June's brothers, Edwin and John. That reunion led to the only time that all three brothers would appear on stage together. Their joint performance would occur at New York's old Winter Garden Theatre in the November 25, 1864 production of *Julius Caesar*. It was advertised as featuring "The Three Sons of the Great Booth" and celebrated the tercentennial of Shakespeare's birth. Confederate sympathizers, determined to burn New York down to the ground during the waning months of the war, frequently set fires in the lower Broadway theater district. The clanging of fire bells could be heard in the midst of Act II when the building next door was set ablaze. Edwin Booth calmed the audience, and the play continued to its conclusion. The proceeds of this joint performance ($3,500) were mainly used to purchase a statue of William Shakespeare, which still stands in New York's Central Park.

While the production of *Julius Caesar* was deemed a great theatrical success for the Booths, it was followed by a furious personal and political quarrel over breakfast at the Booth family home. John insisted that the fires were justified in light of Union army atrocities in the South. Edwin responded that he supported the actions of the Union army, and June added that vigilante justice, comparable to that in San Francisco, was more than justified for the arsonists. When Edwin revealed that he had voted for Lincoln's reelection, John became infuriated and "exclaimed that if the North won the war,

Lincoln would proclaim himself king."[72] Enraged, Edwin banished the equally enraged John from the house.

John Wilkes headed south to Washington, where he performed as the villain, Pescara, in *The Apostate* at Ford's Theatre in March 1865. John was very familiar with Ford's, as he had performed there on several occasions. On the night of April 14, John visited a saloon next door to the theater for some whiskey. A man sitting nearby scornfully commented, "'You'll never be the actor your father was.' Booth smiled and nodded. 'When I leave the stage,' he said quietly, 'I will be the most famous man in America.'"[73]

Laura Keene had left San Francisco in 1856, following the ill-fated tour of Australia with Edwin Booth. In 1857, she opened a theater in New York City, becoming the first female theater owner in the United States. She saw a great deal of potential in an 1853 comedic play, *Our American Cousin*, which, with revisions made by her, became a huge moneymaker and provided a leading role for Keene herself. She would portray that role in the Washington production of the play at Ford's Theatre on the fateful evening of April 14, 1865, for an audience of more than one thousand theater patrons, which included President and Mrs. Lincoln. *Our American Cousin* would be the last production at Ford's Theatre for more than a century, as the comedy became a tragedy during its third act. As it turned out, that mid-April night's performance would be the one during which John Wilkes Booth (who was not in the cast) entered the balcony box occupied by the president (and his party of four) at about 10:15 p.m. and shot Lincoln behind his left ear. The unexpected sharp discharge of his pistol and the screams from Mrs. Lincoln momentarily bewildered the audience and the actors. Spellbound, all eyes watched as Booth jumped eleven and a half feet down onto the theater's stage, shouted out words referencing the revenge of the South and then escaped out a rear stage door to a waiting horse.

Joseph Booth had arrived in San Francisco in early 1864 following a three-year journey traveling the world. After June and his family left the city, he stayed behind, working as a clerk/letter carrier for Wells Fargo. Homesick for his family, Joseph traveled back to the East Coast in mid-April 1865. While en route, he heard the news of Lincoln's assassination and that a man named Booth was the hunted killer. Though details were few, Joseph suspected that the guilty party in question was a member of his immediate family, and he had a pretty good idea who it was.

June and Edwin were performing in Northern cities on the night of the assassination—June in Cincinnati, Edwin in Boston. Having retired for the evening following two performances earlier that day, Edwin would not hear the news until the following morning, when his Negro servant rushed into his bedroom with a copy of the morning newspaper and shook him awake with the news of John Wilke's violent act. Edwin was stunned, as was June when he was informed. After being briefly detained by the police, the brothers returned to the family home in New York City, where they sequestered themselves.

The Booth family feared retaliation following the assassination, and they hoped that John Wilkes would not be taken alive. They did not want to endure the drama and publicity of his capture, trial and presumed execution. Conspiracy theories swirled around the family as June; his sister, Asia; and her husband, John Sleeper Clarke, were each arrested at the direction of Secretary of War Edwin M. Stanton. Letters, documents and other papers seemingly incriminated them. June Booth spent two months in the Old Capitol Prison.[74] John Clarke was imprisoned there for a month, and his wife, Asia, was placed under house arrest. Edwin managed to stay out of prison, thanks to his reputation within theatrical circles and his social connections. A private, casual interview with Assistant Secretary of War Charles Dana removed any suggestion of complicity on Edwin's part. He would never again play Washington, however. In 1873, working with an assistant, Edwin burned John's collection of costumes, wigs and stage props, some of which had belonged to their late father.

Northern newspapers declared that Lincoln was the latest and perhaps final sacrifice on the altar of the Union. A frequent refrain uttered by clergy and "echoed by persons both North and South was that his death was a chastening for an interest in the sinful theater, as the war had been a chastisement for the country's sinful greed."[75] This sentiment was a reflection of an old puritanical belief that theaters were the devil's venue and not a place a president should frequent. Sinful or not, Lincoln enjoyed attending theatrical performances and was long known to be a regular theatergoer, particularly enjoying the works of Shakespeare. In a personal letter written in the summer of 1863, Lincoln noted his admiration of *Macbeth*, a play that could be viewed as symbolically analogous to the tragedy of the Civil War and its aftermath. Often performed in the 1860s, it was a fitting production for the period.

Actors had been welcomed at the Lincoln White House and often performed selected readings for gathered guests. The Lincolns invited John Wilkes Booth himself to a gathering at the White House about three weeks prior to the assassination. Upon being introduced, "the President greeted him very cordially, and taking him by the hand said: 'Mr. Booth, I am proud to meet you as a son of the elder Booth.'"[76]

Telegraphed reports of President Lincoln's assassination spread like wildfire throughout San Francisco and brought the city to a standstill. Only five days had passed since Confederate general Robert E. Lee had surrendered to Union general Ulysses S. Grant. Joyful celebrations marking the end of the war abruptly ended as a somber tone took hold of much of the city. Lincoln's slaying was a shock for West Coast Unionists, particularly those in San Francisco. Banks, saloons and the courts all closed in mourning for the president's death. Businesses across the city quietly locked their doors and shut their shutters. Flags were lowered to half-staff, and bells mournfully tolled throughout the city, prompted by the one at city hall in Portsmouth Square. Guns boomed at Fort Point and from the fort at Alcatraz. Black bands began appearing on the arms and hats of many residents, while black crape was draped on many buildings. An English gentleman visiting San Francisco commented to Isabelle Saxon, a San Francisco resident:

> *I only wonder how they keep so calm. I don't believe I could feel worse if it had been Queen Victoria. And, by heaven! if I was an American, I am afraid I should have shot the first Secessionist I met. A cold-blooded, brutal, dastardly act; I believe it was a madman's; but if it turns out a conspiracy, I can hardly blame the Yankees if they go in for extermination. Some Secessionists have been glorying in the news; if they do that there will be bloodshed here beyond all question.*[77]

San Francisco theaters closed on April 15, the day the news of the assassination reached the city, and again on April 19, the day of Lincoln's funeral services. There would be no performances on either evening, as the city and most of its residents formally mourned the loss of their nation's leader. On the day of the president's funeral, the *Daily Dramatic Chronicle* did not publish.

The solemnity and gloom that had first gripped the city gave way to anger and resentment. An angry Unionist mob descended upon the offices of newspapers that had criticized Lincoln and the Union, destroying their equipment and setting fires. Among those targeted were the offices of the *Democratic Press*, the *News Letter* and the *Monitor*.[78] Mayor Coon had to call on soldiers from the Presidio to restore the peace, and the city was under martial law through the following day. An uncompromising secessionist,

General Henry Halleck (seventh from left) of San Francisco was the only Californian present during the vigil at Lincoln's bedside, witnessing his death at 7:22 a.m. on April 15, 1865. *Courtesy Library of Congress.*

standing on a Montgomery Street corner, angrily told a reporter from the *Daily Alta California*:

> *This is not the assassination of President Lincoln and Secretary Seward only; it is the assassination of the whole South! Damned to the bottomless pit of hell be the men who plotted and carried it out! We had come to look on the restoration of the Union as a foregone conclusion, and the whole South was on the eve of accepting the fact. We should have been friends and brothers once more, but for this, within six months. Now, God help us all!* [79]

Having left San Francisco at the outbreak of the war, General Henry Halleck was among those holding the overnight vigil at the dying Lincoln's bedside on the night of April 15–16. He was the only Californian present to witness the president's death at 7:22 am. Several days later, he served as one of Lincoln's pallbearers.

The use of the telegraph elevated President Lincoln's assassination to a national event. On Easter Sunday, April 16, San Francisco churches held

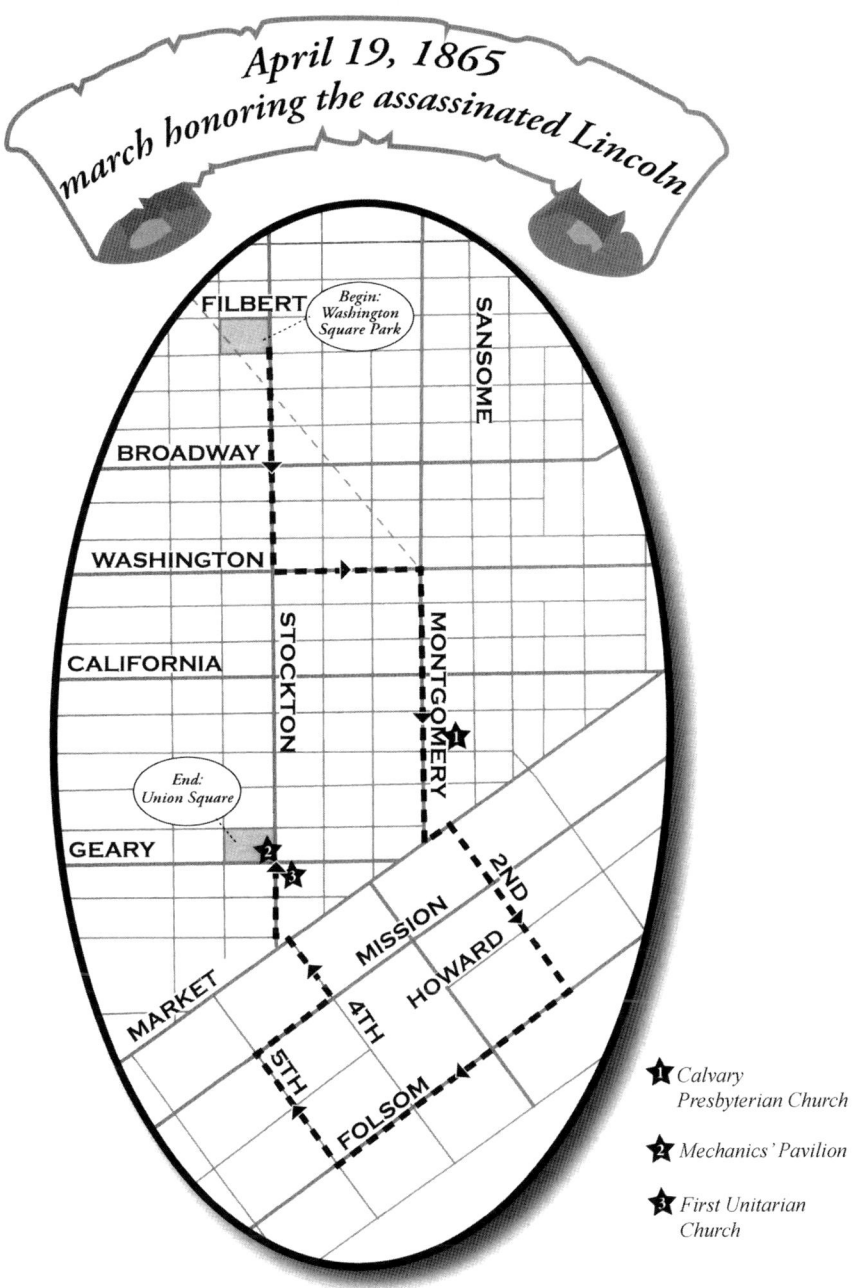

Residents joined soldiers for the march that wound its way to Union Square for San Francisco's public memorial service for the slain president at the Mechanics' Pavilion. *Created and designed by Mary K. Ohliger.*

Lincoln mourners are shown marching down Second Street before turning west on Folsom Street, April 19, 1865. *Courtesy San Francisco History Center, San Francisco Public Library.*

special services memorializing the late president, with the most elaborate held at the First Unitarian Church. On April 19, the city honored Lincoln with its own funeral procession. Led by Mayor Coon, fifteen thousand mourners followed a canopied hearse drawn by six white horses sporting black ostrich plumes. The empty crimson coffin it carried featured the name "Lincoln" in gold gilt lettering.

Chapter 13

Remaining Players

John and Jessie Frémont spent the war years initially in St. Louis but mainly in New York. It was there that they would hear of the deaths of Edward Baker, Reverend Thomas Starr King and Lincoln. Jessie, who had never been a strong supporter of the president and was often critical of his persona, blunders and mismanagement, noted in a letter that his "cruel death silenced much truth."[80] The Frémonts would not return to San Francisco until September 1878, when they briefly occupied a lavish corner suite in the Palace Hotel. They continued on to Los Angeles and the Arizona Territory, where John served as governor until 1881. He died in 1890 in New York City. Jessie lived off John's government pension but was never reimbursed for the loss of their home and property at Black Point. She spent her remaining years living in a cottage in Los Angeles, where she died in 1902 at age seventy-eight.

In mid-1865, the CSS *Shenandoah*, sailing for the Confederacy, was on its way to San Francisco because its captain considered the city as weakly defended. An encounter with a British ship, the *Barracouta*, confirmed that the war had indeed ended several months prior. Disappointed with the Confederacy's collapse, the captain of the *Shenandoah* changed course and set sail for England.

Henry Halleck returned to San Francisco in mid-1865, having been transferred to the Division of the Pacific; he remained in the city until 1869. He was then assigned to command the Military Division of the South, which was headquartered in Louisville, Kentucky.

Archibald Peachy remained in California during the war years and served in the state senate, where he was a member of several important committees. While Billings returned to Vermont in 1866, Peachy stayed on in San Francisco until his death in 1883. The formal partnership of Halleck, Peachy and Billings and its ownership of the Montgomery Block building were actually retained until Halleck's death in 1872. The 1853 Montgomery Block was demolished in 1959 and eventually replaced by the Transamerica Pyramid.

In a particularly bold move, Edwin Booth appropriated Laura Keene's version of *Our American Cousin* and presented it at New York City's old Winter Garden in September 1865. His brother-in-law, John Sleeper Clarke, was featured in the lead male role. Keene was outraged at not having been consulted and sued. She and many others were astounded at Edwin's willingness to profit off the play's notoriety. Edwin, who had for years supported much of the extended Booth family, saw an opportunity both to make money and stage his comeback. He was also determined to repair the family name. In 1869, a brand-new theater built by Booth, the Temple of Dramatic Arts, opened in New York. It featured a bust of Junius Brutus Booth Sr. in the lobby, along with one of William Shakespeare. The theater cost more than twice the estimate to build it, and the economic recession that followed caused the Booth Theater to go dark in 1874. Desperate for money, Edwin responded by doing what his famous father had done: he began traveling the theatrical circuit, taking his connections to the martyred Lincoln and the tragedy of the Civil War to the West.

A grand new theater also opened in San Francisco in 1869: the California on Bush Street. Four years later, it would be the venue for performances of *Our American Cousin*. San Franciscans could then see for themselves the play during which Lincoln met his end.

Edwin's eldest brother, June, returned to San Francisco in 1874 with his third wife, Agnes, for her engagement at the California Theatre. June was ready to retire from the stage and busied himself with the sale of several of his valuable properties in the city. The proceeds were used to build a seaside hotel in Massachusetts. June Booth died there in 1883 at age sixty-one.

Twenty years after his departure, Edwin Booth arrived back in San Francisco in 1876. He enjoyed a particularly successful eight-week run of mainly Shakespearean plays at the California Theatre. The house was packed every night, and hundreds of theatergoers were regularly turned away. Booth received standing ovations following each and every performance. He left the city amply rewarded, just as he had in 1856. Edwin

A Western Theater for Northern & Southern Politics

The 1,600-seat California Theatre was the first theater in the West to use calcium light (limelight) with parabolic reflectors to illuminate the stage. *Courtesy San Francisco History Center, San Francisco Public Library.*

returned to San Francisco on three more occasions during the late 1880s, again performing in Shakespearean plays at the city's Baldwin Theatre. Booth would return to the California Theatre in 1889, performing the role of Iago in *Othello*. It was a part he had first played in the West in December 1852. That performance had taken place in a barn theater as the snow fell on the mining camp that would become Nevada City and where Edwin would learn of his father's death.

During his forty-year acting career, Edwin had clearly outdone his father and his brothers in the theater and was recognized as America's greatest actor of the second half of the nineteenth century. His death in New York City in 1893 at age sixty was regarded by many as the end of the golden age of classical acting in the United States. But despite Edwin's successes and theatrical renown, he would be historically outperformed by his younger brother, John Wilkes. Theater collided with history on the night of April 14, 1865, when John shot the final shot of the war in Ford's Theatre, killing a president who had been both beloved and reviled. During his short life, John, who sought fame through his acting, in the end found only infamy as the world's youngest tragedian. For every one thousand people who knew of Edwin's exploits in the theater, millions more would know of John's.

Edwin Booth's death occurred at just around the time that motion pictures began in the United States. It would take more than sixty years, however, for a movie studio to tell Edwin's story on film. Twentieth Century-Fox did so in a 1955 production entitled *Prince of Players*, a feature film, not a documentary. Richard Burton would perform the role of Edwin and Raymond Massey that of his father, Junius Sr. The film includes their time in San Francisco. Edwin's tale couldn't be told, however, without bringing in the character of John Wilkes Booth, who was suitably portrayed by John Derek. In his *New York Times* review, film critic Bosley Crowther noted that "Derek's playacting as John Wilkes is aptly flashy and grandiloquent."[81]

During June Booth's thirteen years in San Francisco, he and his family lived in a house on Calhoun Street up on Telegraph Hill. The Hill attracted many people connected with the theater, becoming San Francisco's first bohemian colony. Laura Keene lived on the Hill during her two years in San Francisco. Also on Calhoun Street was the home of Dr. David "Yankee" Robinson, the theater entrepreneur. In the 1920s, Booth's house tumbled down the eastern slope of the Hill, rendered unstable by many years of relentless quarrying and dynamiting by the Gray Brothers Crushed Rock Company. Robinson's two-story house, dating back to 1854 and featuring Carpenter Gothic detailing, survives and is the oldest house on the street. It's also one of the oldest up on the Hill.

For three decades, Tom Maguire successfully attracted top-caliber actors to the city and was regarded by many as the "Napoleon of the San Francisco Stage." Maguire remained active in San Francisco theatrical circles until 1882. He ended his days in the city as the manager of the Baldwin Theatre. After thirty-five years of owning and managing theaters in San Francisco, he returned to New York City, where he died in 1896. As with so many who worked in the theater, Maguire became impoverished in his later years and financially dependent on the Actors Fund.

William Gwin, whose term as senator had ended in the spring of 1861, then left California, intending to offer his services to Jefferson Davis. He was arrested and imprisoned upon arrival in New York, mainly for his treasonable comments and behavior during the voyage, whose passengers included General Sumner. Though viewed as a secessionist sympathizer

This 1854 house was occupied by theater impresario and playwright Dr. David G. "Yankee" Robinson until 1856. It's one of the oldest residences on Telegraph Hill. *Courtesy of the author.*

by the Lincoln administration, particularly Secretary of State Seward, President Lincoln intervened for his release. Gwin sent his wife and younger daughter to Europe while he, himself, headed down to his plantation in Mississippi. Unfortunately, Gwin's property was positioned on the route General Grant took for the Union army's attack on Vicksburg in 1863. His plantation was burned to the ground, and Gwin lost his home and all his papers. He reunited with his family in Paris, where he ran into Thomas Butler King. King was there to remind the European powers of the value of maintaining commerce with the Southern states. Gwin tried to interest Napoleon III in an anti-Union plot that included resettling American slaveholders in Sonora, Mexico. The scheme fell apart, and in 1865, Gwin returned to the United States, only to be arrested in New Orleans as per Secretary Seward. Gwin was imprisoned in Mississippi until President Andrew Johnson ordered his release. Gwin and his family made their way back to San Francisco, where he lived out his life, engaging in mining and agricultural investments. Gwin died in 1885 at age seventy-nine. Despite Gwin's participation as a delegate to the 1849 California Constitutional Convention, his many years of residency in San Francisco, his service as a two-term senator representing California in Congress and his continual advocacy for the transcontinental railroad, there are no streets in San Francisco named for Senator Gwin or any monuments honoring him.

California senator William M. Gwin was interred in this private family mausoleum in Mountain View Cemetery in Oakland, California. *Courtesy of the author.*

A Western Theater for Northern & Southern Politics

Combative to the end of his life, David Terry finally met his due. Returning to California in 1869, he settled in Stockton. Thirty years after the Broderick-Terry duel, Terry was once again involved in a public mêlée. He disagreed with a circuit court ruling made by U.S. Supreme Court justice Stephen J. Field that had to do with a contentious divorce case involving Terry. Field, who had served in the California state assembly in the 1850s, had been a strong supporter of David Broderick. It was Field who had replaced Terry as California's chief justice in 1859. In 1889, during a chance encounter with Justice Field at a railroad station in the Central Valley town of Lathrop, Terry publicly slapped Field in the back of his head and then in the face. Field's bodyguard shot Terry dead on the spot. David Terry had at long last received his comeuppance.

Ulysses S. Grant planned to reside in California following the end of the Civil War, but as it turned out, he would only return to the West Coast for visits. After a twenty-five-year absence, the former President Grant and his wife, Julia, paid a visit to San Francisco in the autumn of 1879. The great Civil War general, apparently untouched by the scandals of his presidential administration, was warmly welcomed and cheered by the citizens of San Francisco. The Grants were honored at a grand reception at the Palace Hotel.

Although Sam Brannan was the head of the Mormon Church in California beginning in 1846, many Mormons were unhappy with his leadership. They accused him of diverting church tithes toward his own business ventures and complained about him to Governor Mason and then-lieutenant Sherman. Both advised them to cease payments of tithes to Brannan. Most did so. But failure to account for already-collected monies combined with his increasing alcoholism caused Brannan to be officially removed as both an elder and a member of the Mormon Church. An outspoken Unionist, his judgment during the Civil War years would be clouded by his growing alcoholism. He subsequently lost his businesses, his wife divorced him and his friends abandoned him. Brannan eventually drifted down to Southern California, where he died penniless in a lonely attic room in Escondido in 1889. He was seventy. Millions of dollars had passed through Sam Brannan's hands during his years in San Francisco, and in the end, there were no funds left to bury him. Neglected and forgotten, his body lay unclaimed for more than a year. He would eventually be buried in a San Diego cemetery.

The *Daily Alta California*, which dated back to 1849 and which began, in part, as the *California Star* under the auspices of Sam Brannan, published its final edition in June 1891.

William T. Sherman returned to San Francisco in 1876 for a brief visit but lived the rest of his life in New York City, where he pursued his love of theater, amateur painting and, as a popular speaker, frequently quoting Shakespeare. In addition to his 1875 memoirs, Sherman wrote articles. One was about his days in the West and entitled "Old Times in California," published in the March 1889 issue of the *North American Review*. In it, Sherman commented, "The existence of San Francisco on the Pacific coast was demanded by the civilization of the whole world—a necessary link between Europe, America, Japan, China, etc. Mexico was not equal to accomplish this task…" Sherman declined a nomination as the Republican candidate for president in 1884 and died in New York in 1891.

During her fifty years in San Francisco, Mary Ellen Pleasant was a witness to sweeping changes that occurred in the city and in the nation. Following the war, Pleasant changed her designation in the San Francisco City Directory from "white" to "black," causing a bit of a stir amid both groups. As a black woman of that era, Pleasant both benefitted from and was victimized by the changing landscape and social mores. While she earned the title of the mother of the civil rights movement in California, she was often mischaracterized as a voodoo priestess, a madam and a baby stealer, among other things. Most unfairly, she had the misnomer of "mammy" attached to her name. She was many things in her lifetime—a capitalist, an abolitionist, a philanthropist, a litigant—but she was never a mammy, and she spent her later years correcting those who labeled her as such. Pleasant made and lost a fortune during her years in the West and died in poverty in San Francisco in early 1904. She was approximately ninety years old and took the secrets of her origins with her to her grave.

Lillie Hitchcock translated war reports for Napoleon III in France during the war. She would also be a foreign correspondent for San Francisco's *Evening Bulletin* while remaining a supporter of the Southern cause. While in Paris, Lillie and her mother, Martha, heard of the Confederacy's surrender followed by Lincoln's assassination. Lillie was shocked by the news and then aghast when, shortly thereafter, she attended a dinner populated by displaced Southerners, who heartily celebrated Lincoln's death with multiple toasts and by dancing jigs.

In the 1920s, she lived at San Francisco's Fairmont Hotel on Nob Hill, enjoying views of the modern metropolis the city had become. Her health failing and paralyzed by a stroke, Lillie Hitchcock Coit was moved to the Dante Sanatorium on Russian Hill, where she died in July 1929. She was eighty-seven years old.[82]

Mary Ellen Pleasant at approximately eighty-seven years of age, 1901. Following her death in San Francisco in 1904, Pleasant was buried in Napa, California. *Courtesy San Francisco History Center, San Francisco Public Library*.

Antebellum and Civil War San Francisco

In 1927, this statue of Lincoln was placed on the lawn of San Francisco's city hall by "the Lincoln Monument League representing the Grand Army of the Republic & the Lincoln Grammar School Association of San Francisco." *Courtesy of the author.*

Using funds left to the city by Mrs. Coit, an elegant, fluted tower now known as Coit Tower was built on the summit of Telegraph Hill. It was dedicated to the memory of "fire belle Lillie" on October 8, 1933. In her honor, the old Knickerbocker Engine #5 was once more brought up to the top of the Hill on that autumn day.

Throughout and following the antebellum and Civil War eras, San Francisco continued to strengthen its connection to the East through the use of the Pony Express, the telegraph and, beginning in 1869, the transcontinental railroad. After years of arduous journeys by land and by sea, the railroad would shorten travel to San Francisco from New York to one week, ending the West's geographic isolation.

President Lincoln spoke of California as a potential future home after his second term ended. He enjoyed hearing stories about the West and often stated that he longed to see it, especially San Francisco and the Pacific Ocean. He never would.

The reporting of Lincoln's assassination began the transformation of the afternoon *Daily Dramatic Chronicle* into the *Morning Chronicle* (renamed in 1868). The de Young brothers[83] stated that this new *Chronicle* would be "a bright, bold, fearless and truly independent paper."[84] A year later, it would become known as the *San Francisco Chronicle*, "The Voice of the West." Included on the *Daily Dramatic Chronicle*'s secondary masthead (found on the newspaper's second page) in April 1865 were the prophetic words of William Shakespeare:

All the world's a stage,
And all the men and women merely players.[85]

The End.

Appendix

Sites and Streets Related to the Antebellum and Civil War Eras in San Francisco

* = discussed in the narrative

SITES
(All sites are in San Francisco unless otherwise noted.)

Alcatraz/Angel Islands*

Black Point/Fort Mason*

Broderick-Terry Duel site*

California Star newspaper office site* (plaque)

Civil War Memorial Grove, Capitol Park, Sacramento—composed of trees from major Civil War battle sites and a statue of Reverend Thomas Starr King (formerly in Statuary Hall)

Coit Tower* (Lillie Hitchcock)

Colton Hall, Monterey*

Fort "Gunnybags"* (plaque)

Fort Point/Golden Gate Straits*

Haskell House*

Jenny Lind Theatre/City Hall site* (plaque)

Larkin House, Monterey*

Appendix

Niantic site* (plaque)

Old Clam House, The*

Old Ship Saloon, The*

Pleasant* Memorial Park and sidewalk plaque

Portsmouth Square*

Presidio*

Robinson, Dr. David "Yankee" residence*

Sherman's Bank building*

Statues honoring: Ulysses S. Grant*, Henry W. Halleck*, Abraham Lincoln*, Hall McAllister* and Thomas Starr King*

Tadich Grill*

Union Cemetery, Redwood City

Union Square*

United States Mint* 1854–1874 (plaque)

About forty Union soldiers are buried in San Francisco Peninsula's Union Cemetery. The inscription on the monument reads: "To the memory of Californias [*sic*] patriotic dead who served during the war for the Union. Mustered out." *Courtesy of the author.*

Appendix

Streets

Anderson Street: Union general Robert Anderson

Armistead Road: Confederate general Lewis Armistead; commanded Presidio in 1859, killed at Gettysburg

Baker Street: Edward D. Baker*

Beale Street: Edward F. Beale*

Bluxome Street: Isaac Bluxome, businessman/secretary of 1851/1856 Vigilance Committees

Brannan Street: Sam Brannan*

Broderick Street: David Broderick*

Brooklyn Alley: Brannan's ship*

Burnett Avenue: Peter Burnett*

Calhoun Street/Terrace: John C. Calhoun*

Chapman Street: Union general George Chapman

Chattanooga Street: 1863 Civil War battle

Clay Street: Henry Clay*

Dixie Alley: named for the eleven Southern states that formed the Confederacy

Ellis Street: Alfred Ellis*

Fillmore Street: Millard Fillmore*

Folsom Street: Joseph Folsom*

Fremont Street: John C. Frémont*

Geary Street/Boulevard: John W. Geary*

Gilbert Street: Edward Gilbert*

Grant Avenue: Ulysses S. Grant*

Halleck Street: Henry Halleck*

Jones Street: Elbert Jones*

King Street: Thomas Butler King*

Larkin Street: Thomas Larkin*

Appendix

Lee Avenue: Lieutenant Custis Lee, U.S. Army's Department of California, 1850s (son of Confederate general Robert E. Lee)

Lincoln Boulevard/Way/Court: Abraham Lincoln*

Lyon Street: Union general Nathaniel Lyon; first general to be killed in the Civil War

Mason Street: Richard Mason*

McAllister Street: Hall McAllister*

Meade Avenue: Union general George Meade

Montgomery Street: John Montgomery*

Pierce Street: Franklin Pierce*

Pleasant Street: Mary Ellen Pleasant*

Polk Street: James K. Polk*

Prentiss Street: Union general Benjamin Prentiss

Riley Avenue: Bennet Riley*

Scott Street: Winfield Scott*

Seward Street: William Seward*

Sherman Street/Road: William Tecumseh Sherman*

Sloat Boulevard: John Sloat*

Stanford Street: Leland Stanford*

Starr King Drive: Thomas Starr King*

Steuart Street: William Steuart*

Stevenson Street: Jonathan Drake Stevenson*

Taylor Street: Zachary Taylor*

Vicksburg Street: 1863 Civil War battle/siege

Webster Street: Daniel Webster*

Whipple Avenue: Union general Amiel Whipple; died during 1863 battle at Chancellorsville

Wright Loop/Street: Brigadier General George Wright; commander of the Department of the Pacific (1862–64), commander of the District of California (1864–65)

Notes

Chapter 1

1. *Daily Alta California*, April 16, 2014, 1.
2. As noted on the *Daily Dramatic Chronicle*'s masthead (page 2) for April 15, 1865. (According the 1860 U.S. Census, San Francisco's population was just under 57,000. See Hansen, *San Francisco Almanac*, 2).
3. The *Daily Dramatic Chronicle* did not publish on Sundays; Sunday, April 16, was Easter Sunday. Booth's image appeared on page 2 of the Monday edition and was noted to be an engraving "taken from a photograph by Sillsby & Case of Boston, drawn on wood by Edward Jump, and engraved in two hours by Mr. Keith for the *Dramatic Chronicle*." *Daily Dramatic Chronicle*, April 17, 1865, 2.

Chapter 2

4. Kimmel, *Mad Booths of Maryland*, 340. Altogether, there were ten Booth children, though only six survived to adulthood.
5. The San Francisco branch of the St. Louis–based bank was run by Sherman from 1853 to 1857.

Chapter 3

6. Del Matier, McIntosh and Waters, *Rumble of California Politics*, 6–7. Racist policies continued on into the 1850s and '60s as more laws limiting the rights of blacks were passed.

Chapter 4

7. During the Spanish and Mexican eras, it was known as *La Boca de Puerto de San Francisco*.
8. According to the *California Star*, the breakdown as of March 18, 1848, was "575 males, 177 females, 60 children totaling 812 white population." Hansen, *San Francisco Almanac*, 2.
9. Fire was a constant concern, so brick became the preferred choice, though not all brick buildings were fireproof. Many of the brick buildings would add iron shutters to their windows as well.
10. Scherer, *First Forty-Niner*, 83–84.
11. Ashbury. *Barbary Coast*, 11.
12. Briscoe, *Tadich Grill*. The Coffee Stand eventually evolved into the Tadich Grill, which relocated around the Financial District no less than eight times. It's been in its current location since 1967.
13. The brick building currently on the site replaced the one built in 1859, which was destroyed in the 1906 earthquake and fire. Formerly a sailors' tavern and a longtime drinking establishment in what is now the Jackson Square district, the Old Ship Saloon became a full-service restaurant in the late 1990s. See www.oldshipsaloon.com.
14. The first Metropolitan Theatre opened in 1853 and was destroyed by fire in 1857. The replacement theater building opened in 1861 on the same site. In 1873, it was razed to make room for the new Montgomery Avenue, renamed Columbus Avenue in 1909.
15. Ethington, *Public City*, 65.
16. Gaer, *Theater of the Gold Rush*, 5.
17. Until the 1880s, chicken eggs were all but impossible to get in San Francisco, so murre eggs, regarded as rather tasty, were a good substitute. Not so good for the murres, however, as the poaching of their eggs practically wiped out their existence on the Farallons by the turn of the century. See Briscoe, *Tadich Grill*, 20. (Millions of murre eggs would be gathered from the Farallons through the early 1880s. Fierce competition among "eggers" would lead to an egg war in 1863.)
18. Lingering Puritanical beliefs caused some theater owners to call their theaters "museums" in the hopes of making them seemingly innocuous.
19. Jenny Lind was a nineteenth-century Swedish opera singer who became known as the Swedish Nightingale. Lind toured the East Coast of the United States from 1850 to 1852 but never visited San Francisco or the West.

Notes to Pages 35–62

20. Michael (M.H.) officially joined the *Chronicle* in September 1866.
21. Kohler opened the Blue Wing Saloon at 526 Montgomery Street.
22. Richards, *California Gold Rush*, 180.

Chapter 5

23. Founded in 1833, the Whig Party supported commercial growth and opposed continental expansion. The Whigs denounced the war with Mexico, the acquisition of new territories and particularly the expansion of slavery, an issue that could threaten party harmony and did so.
24. Ironically, in 1853, Representative Inge would be appointed by President Franklin Pierce as U.S. attorney for the Northern District of California. Inge died in San Francisco in 1868.
25. Richards, *California Gold Rush*, 105.
26. Ethington, *Public City*, 49.

Chapter 6

27. Stellman, *Sam Brannon*, 64.
28. Richards, *California Gold Rush*, 67.
29. Edward Kemble went back to New York, returning to California in 1857 and becoming associate editor for the *Sacramento Union*. During the Civil War, he would be the war correspondent for the *Union*.
30. Dennison's was located across from Portsmouth Square and would be replaced by the Union Hotel.
31. Pleasant's money was mixed with that from other blacks, and perhaps even some whites, in San Francisco. Secrecy surrounding the planning and funding of Brown's activities and Pleasant's own actions in 1858–59 make it difficult to completely determine who donated to what.
32. Del Matier, McIntosh and Waters, *Rumble of California Politics*, 6–7.
33. Pleasant's husband was the cook on the *Orizaba*.

Chapter 7

34. Later that year, Lippitt, Norton and Gwin would serve as delegates to the Constitutional Convention in Monterey.

Chapter 8

35. Now known as Virginia City, Nevada.

Chapter 9

36. Denton, *Passion and Principle*, 243.
37. Brands, *Age of Gold*, 368.
38. Washington was the great-great-grand nephew of George Washington. In 1863, he would become editor of the pro-Confederacy *Democratic Press*, the predecessor of the *Evening Examiner*, which, after being purchased by George Hearst, would become the *San Francisco Examiner*.
39. Ethington, *Public City*, 176.
40. Terry would be named chief justice in 1857.
41. Matthews, *Golden State in the Civil War*, 26.
42. The terms of the duel were arranged by Broderick's and Terry's seconds and precisely drawn up in the form of nine points.
43. *Daily Alta California*, "The Duellers Arrested," September 13, 1859.
44. Burke arrived armed with warrants obtained from authorities in both San Francisco and San Mateo Counties.
45. *Daily Alta California*, "The Duel—Broderick Shot," September 14, 1859.
46. *San Francisco Times*, "Affair of Honor!" September 14, 1859.
47. *Daily Alta California*, "Death of Senator Broderick," September 17, 1859.
48. The ghostly images of three black adults have also been sighted.
49. Lynch, *A Senator of the Fifties* (oration of Colonel Edward D. Baker), 232–34.

Chapter 10

50. Matthews, *Golden State in the Civil War*, 90–91.
51. May 20, 1860 letter to Randolph Ryer, a freed New England–based black man and longtime friend of King's, to whom he wrote frequently. King Letters and Papers, Bancroft Library, Berkeley, CA.
52. For the full text of Baker's speech, see Vandenhoff, *Edward Dickinson Baker*, 86–95.
53. Richards, *California Gold Rush*, 176, 228.

54. Other Bay Area counties that supported Lincoln were Marin, Contra Costa, Alameda and Santa Clara, plus the counties of Monterey, Santa Cruz, Nevada and San Bernardino. San Mateo County supported Douglas, while Sonoma, Napa and Solano Counties supported Breckinridge. See Del Matier, McIntosh and Waters, *Rumble of California Politics*, 51–52.
55. In comparison, Los Angeles, then a city of approximately 4,400, cast almost 40.0 percent of its vote for Breckinridge. Lincoln received just 20.0 percent and Douglas, 28.5 percent. Los Angeles would remain supportive of the Southern cause throughout the Civil War. See Matthews, *Golden State in the Civil War*, 82.
56. Monzingo, *Thomas Starr King*, 61.
57. Sherman, *Memoirs*, 152.
58. Herr, *Jessie Benton Fremont*, 317.
59. Matthews, *Golden State in the Civil War*, 99.

Chapter 11

60. Fort Point was part of the U.S. Army's Third System of military architecture adopted in 1820. "While there were more than 30 such forts on the East Coast, Fort Point was the only one of its type built on the West Coast." See www.nps.gov/goga/historyculture/fort-point.htm.
61. Shortly after California became part of the United States, the island was nicknamed the "Battleship in the Bay." See Martini, *Fortress Alcatraz*, 5.
62. John Wilkes Booth was an early member of the Baltimore chapter and would draw on his KGC connections for assistance and favors for his schemes.
63. California, Oregon and the Washington and Utah Territories.
64. The western territories consisted of Washington, Utah (which included much of present-day Nevada and a portion of present-day Colorado and present-day Wyoming) and New Mexico (which included present-day Arizona). See *Lincoln and California*, "Politics 1860."
65. In 1940, his remains were moved to San Francisco National Cemetery in the Presidio.
66. *Mr. Lincoln's T-mails*, p. xvii.
67. Richards, *California Gold Rush*, 229–34.
68. Mason and Frémont had come close to dueling in 1847 when Mason replaced Frémont as governor.

69. In 1889, the First Unitarian Church relocated to Franklin Street, where it is today. Reverend King's sarcophagus was reinterred in its front courtyard. A statue of him surrounded by children stands nearby. The City of Paris department store was built at the church's Geary/Stockton location in 1896 and remained there until 1980. It was replaced by the current Neiman-Marcus store.
70. The Reverend King's importance to California's history and development was demonstrated when a bronze statue of him was one of two placed at Statuary Hall in Washington, D.C. in 1931 to represent California. In 2009, King's statue was removed and replaced by one of former president Ronald Reagan. King's statue now stands in the Civil War Memorial Grove on the grounds of the California State Capitol in Sacramento.
71. The *Comanche* limped along until 1899, when it was sold for scrap. It never justified the cost of its construction, delivery or salvage and became obsolete as larger, more powerful postwar ironclads were built. See www.trampsofsanfrancisco.com/comanche.

Chapter 12

72. Kimmel, *Mad Booths of Maryland*, 193.
73. Bishop, *The Day Lincoln Was Shot*, 204.
74. Built for Congress as a temporary capitol following the War of 1812, the Old Capitol building eventually became a prison for Confederate soldiers during the Civil War. A number of people connected with the Lincoln assassination were held at this prison, including John T. Ford, the owner of Ford's Theatre. The building was torn down in 1929 and is now the site of the U.S. Supreme Court building.
75. Henneke, *Laura Keene*, 215.
76. Taylor, "A New Story of the Assassination of Lincoln," 302.
77. Isabelle Saxon, "An Englishwoman's View of the War" in *More San Francisco Memoirs*, 151.
78. *Daily Alta California*, "Mob Violence," April 16, 1865, 1.
79. *Daily Alta California*, "City Items: The Feeling of Southern Men," April 16, 1865, 1. (Secretary of State William Seward actually survived the attempt on his life by Booth co-conspirator Lewis Powell.)

Chapter 13

80. Herr, *Jessie Benton Fremont*, 375.
81. *New York Times*, "'Prince of Players' Bows at the Rivoli," January 12, 1955.
82. Lillie Hitchcock Coit was buried in the Hitchcock family mausoleum in Cypress Lawn Cemetery (Colma, CA). The former Dante Sanitarium is now the Notre Dame Apartments (Broadway and Van Ness Avenue). Lillie left one-third of her estate to the city of San Francisco; $5,000 was designated for each member of the Knickerbocker #5 Fire Company who survived her. Three members did so.
83. Gustavus de Young left the paper in the mid-1870s and was eventually committed to the Stockton State Insane Asylum. As reported in the *San Francisco Call*, he died there on October 11, 1906. Charles de Young was shot dead in his office in 1880. Michael (M.H.) de Young outlived his brother, Charles, by forty-five years, continuing to publish the *Chronicle*. In 1894, he founded the museum that evolved into the de Young Museum, located in Golden Gate Park.
84. *San Francisco Chronicle*, "134 Years of the *Chronicle*," June 16, 1999.
85. Quote concludes: "They have their exits and their entrances; And one man in his time plays many parts." *As You Like It*, Act II, Scene VII.

Bibliography

Ashbury, Herbert. *The Barbary Coast*. New York: Alfred A. Knopf, 1933.
Barbey, John. "Folsom: The Scoundrel." *New Mission News*, September 1992.
Barker, Malcolm E., ed. *More San Francisco Memoirs: 1852–1899*. San Francisco, CA: Londonborn Publications, 1996.
Berson, Misha. *The San Francisco Stage: From Gold Rush to Golden Spike, 1849-1869*, published by The San Francisco Performing Arts Library and Museum (PALM), No. 2, Fall 1989.
Bishop, James A. *The Day Lincoln Was Shot*. New York: Harper, 1955.
Brands, H.W. *The Age of Gold: The California Gold Rush and the New American Dream*. New York: Doubleday, 2002.
Brechin, Gray. *Imperial San Francisco: Urban Power, Earthly Ruin*. Berkeley: University of California Press, 1999.
Briscoe, John. *Tadich Grill: The Story of San Francisco's Oldest Restaurant*. Berkeley, CA: Ten Speed Press, 2002.
Burchfield, Christopher. *Choose Your Weapon: The Duel in California*. Seattle, WA: Stairway Press, 2013.
Cash, Bill. "Abraham Lincoln and John Bright: A Special Relationship." www.newstatesman.com.
Clauss, Francis J. *Angel Island: Jewel of San Francisco Bay*. Menlo Park, CA: Briarcliff Press, 1982.
Conway, J.D. *Monterey: Presidio, Pueblo, and Port*. Charleston, SC: Arcadia Publishing, 2003.
Cooper, William J., Jr. *Jefferson Davis and the Civil War Years*. Baton Rouge: Louisiana State University Press, 2008.

Bibliography

Daily Alta California. April 16, 1865 (all front-page articles).

Delmatier, Royce D., Clarence F. McIntosh and Earl G. Waters, eds. *The Rumble of California Politics: 1848–1970.* New York: John Wiley & Sons, 1970.

Denton, Sally. *Passion and Principle: John and Jessie Frémont, the Couple Whose Power, Politics, and Love Shaped Nineteenth-Century America.* New York: Bloomsbury USA, 2007.

Eames, David B. *San Francisco Street Secrets: The Stories Behind San Francisco's Street Names.* Baldwin Park, CA: Gem Guides Book Company, 1995.

Ellington, Charles G. *The Trial of U.S. Grant: The Pacific Coast Years, 1852–1854.* Glendale, CA: Arthur H. Clark Company, 1987.

Ellison, William Henry. *A Self-Governing Dominion: California, 1849–1860.* Berkeley: University of California Press, 1950.

Estavan, Lawrence, ed. *San Francisco Theater Research: Monographs.* WPA Project. Volumes 2, 4 and 6. August 1938.

Ethington, Philip J. *The Public City: The Political Construction of Urban Life in San Francisco, 1850–1900.* New York: Cambridge University Press, 1994.

Fracchia, Charles A. *The Golden Dream: Gold Rush to Statehood.* Portland, OR: Graphic Arts Center Publishers, 1997.

———. *When the Water Came Up to Montgomery Street.* Virginia Beach, VA: Donning Company Publishers, 2009.

Gaer, Joseph, ed. *The Theatre of the Gold Rush Decade of San Francisco.* New York: Burt Franklin, 1935.

Gagey, Edmond M. *The San Francisco Stage: A History.* New York: Columbia University Press, 1950.

Goodman, Dean. *San Francisco Stages: A Concise History, 1849–1986.* San Francisco, CA: Micro Pro Litera Press, 1986.

Hague, Harlan, and David J. Langum. *Thomas O. Larkin: A Life of Patriotism and Profit in Old California.* Norman: University of Oklahoma Press, 1990.

Hansen, Gladys. *San Francisco Almanac.* San Rafael, CA: Presidio Press, 1980.

Henneke, Ben Graf. *Laura Keene: Actress, Innovator and Impresario.* Tulsa, OK: Council Oak Books, 1990.

Herr, Pamela. *Jessie Benton Fremont: American Woman of the 19th Century.* New York: Franklin Watts, 1987.

Hogan, William, and William German, eds. *The San Francisco Chronicle Reader.* New York: McGraw-Hill, 1962.

Holdredge, Helen. *Firebelle Lillie: The Life and Times of Lillie Coit of San Francisco.* New York: Meredith Press, 1967.

Hudson, Lynn. *The Making of "Mammy Pleasant": A Black Entrepreneur in Nineteenth-Century San Francisco.* Chicago: University of Illinois Press, 2003.

Bibliography

Jones, Idwal. *Ark of Empire: San Francisco's Montgomery Block*. Garden City, NY: Doubleday & Company, 1951.

Josephy, Alvin M., Jr. *The Civil War in the American West*. New York: Alfred A. Knopf, 1991.

Kamiya, Gary. "1850s San Francisco Rallied to Free a Slave." *San Francisco Chronicle*, January 10, 2014.

———. "No Summer of Love in S.F.'s Vigilante Days." *San Francisco Chronicle*, December 27, 2013.

Keehn, David C. *Knights of the Golden Circle: Secret Empire, Southern Secession, Civil War*. Baton Rouge: Louisiana State University Press, 2013.

Kennedy, Elijah R. *The Contest for California in 1861: How Colonel E.D. Baker Saved the Pacific States to the Union*. Boston: Houghton Mifflin Company, 1912.

Kimmel, Stanley. *The Mad Booths of Maryland*. New York: Dover Publications, 1940.

Lamar, Howard R., ed. *The Reader's Encyclopedia of the American West*. New York: Harper & Row, 1977.

Levine, Bruce. *The Fall of the House of Dixie: The Civil War and the Social Revolution That Transformed the South*. New York: Random House, 2013.

"Lincoln and the West: The Legacy of the Lincoln Administration in the American West." Seminar sponsored by the Bill Lane Center for the American West, Stanford University, February 5–6, 2009.

Loewenstein, Louis K. *Streets of San Francisco: The Origins of Street and Place Names*. Berkeley, CA: Wilderness Press, 1996.

Lotchin, Roger W. *San Francisco, 1846–1856: From Hamlet to City*. New York: Oxford University Press, 1974.

Lynch, Jeremiah. *A Senator of the Fifties: David C. Broderick of California*. San Francisco, CA: A.M. Robertson, 1911.

Martini, John A. *Fortress Alcatraz: Guardian of the Golden Gate*. Kailua, HI: Pacific Monograph, 1990.

Matthews, Glenna. *The Golden State in the Civil War*. New York: Cambridge University Press, 2012.

Media Museum of Northern California. "Edward Kemble." http://www.norcalmediamuseum.com/index.php?option=com_content&view=article&id=96&Itemid=116.

Monzingo, Robert. *Thomas Starr King: Eminent Californian, Civil War Statesman, Unitarian Minister*. Pacific Grove, CA: Boxwood Press, 1991.

Mullen, Kevin J. *Let Justice Be Done: Crime and Politics in Early San Francisco*. Reno: University of Nevada Press, 1989.

Neville, Amelia Ransome. *The Fantastic City: Memoirs of the Social and Romantic Life of Old San Francisco*. Boston: Houghton Mifflin Company, 1932.

Bibliography

Nolte, Carl. "134 Years of the *Chronicle*." *San Francisco Chronicle*, June 16, 1999.
Oxford, June. "Firebelle Lillie." *San Francisco Magazine* (August 1976).
Peterson, Richard H. "San Francisco's Fallen Starr: The Death and Legacy of Thomas Starr King in California, 1860–64." *The Argonaut* 5, no. 1 (Spring 1994).
Phillips, Catherine Coffin. *Portsmouth Plaza: The Cradle of San Francisco*. San Francisco, CA: John Henry Nash, 1932.
Quinn, Arthur. *The Rivals: William Gwin, David Broderick and the Birth of California*. New York: Crown Publishers, 1994.
Rather, Lois. *Jessie Frémont at Black Point*. Oakland, CA: Rather Press, 1974.
Richards, Leonard L. *The California Gold Rush and the Coming of the Civil War*. New York: Alfred A. Knopf, 2007.
Richards, Rand, comp. and ed. *Haunted San Francisco: Ghost Stories from the City's Past*. San Francisco, CA: Heritage House Publishers, 2004.
Robinson, John W. *Los Angeles in Civil War Days: 1860–1865*. Norman: University of Oklahoma Press, 2013.
Samples, Gordon. *Lust for Fame: The Stage Career of John Wilkes Booth*. Jefferson, NC: McFarland & Company, 1982.
The San Francisco Chronicle and Its History: 1865–1879. San Francisco, CA, 1879.
Scherer, James A.B. *The First Forty-Niner and the Story of the Golden Tea-Caddy*. New York: Minton, Balch & Company, 1925.
———. *Thirty-First Star*. New York: G.P. Putnam's Sons, 1942.
Schussler, Hermann. *The Locality of the Broderick-Terry Duel on September 13, 1859*. San Francisco, CA: Printed for the Historic Landmarks Committee of the Native Sons of the Golden West by John Henry Nash, 1916.
Sherman, General William T. *Memoirs of General William T. Sherman*. Bloomington: Indiana University Press, 1957.
———. *Recollections of California: 1846–1861*. Oakland, CA: Biobooks, 1945.
Shutes, Milton H. *Lincoln and California*. Stanford, CA: Stanford University Press, 1943.
Smith, Gene. *American Gothic: The Story of America's Legendary Theatrical Family—Junius, Edwin and John Wilkes Booth*. New York: Simon & Schuster, 1992.
Steel, Edward M., Jr. *T. Butler King of Georgia*. Athens: University of Georgia Press, 1964.
Stellman, Louis J. *Sam Brannan: Builder of San Francisco*. New York: Exposition Press, 1953.
Stewart, George R. *Committee of Vigilance: Revolution in San Francisco, 1851*. Boston: Houghton Mifflin Company, 1964.
Taylor, Bayard. *Eldorado: Adventures in the Path of Empire*. New York: George P. Putnam, 1850.

Bibliography

Taylor, W.H. "A New Story of the Assassination of Lincoln." *Leslie's Weekly* 106, March 26, 1908.

Titone, Nora. *My Thoughts Be Bloody: The Bitter Rivalry Between Edwin Booth and John Wilkes Booth That Led to an American Tragedy*. New York: Free Press, 2010.

Vandenhoff, Anne. *Edward Dickinson Baker: Western Gentleman, Frontier Lawyer, American Statesman*. Auburn, CA: self-published, 1979.

Wheeler, Tom. *Mr. Lincoln's T-Mails: How Abraham Lincoln Used the Telegraph to Win the Civil War*. New York: Collins, 2006.

Index

A

Alcatraz 88, 90, 92, 100, 105, 129
Alta California 19, 20, 21, 23, 24, 27, 40, 41, 42, 49, 88
American Theatre 15, 34, 35, 56, 83, 96
Angel Island 89

B

Baker, Edward D. 60, 77, 82, 84, 96, 100, 109
Baker, Lafayette C. 67
Beale, Edward 19, 87
Black Point 76, 80, 87, 98, 109
blacks 23, 38, 49, 54, 58, 59, 98
Booth, Edwin 12, 15, 16, 17, 32, 35, 84, 102, 103, 104, 110, 112
Booth, John Wilkes 10, 12, 14, 17, 59, 84, 101, 103, 104, 111
Booth, Joseph 94, 103
Booth, Junius Brutus 12, 13, 14, 17, 110, 112
Booth, Junius "June" 12, 15, 16, 17, 35, 67, 84, 94, 102, 103, 104, 110, 112
Brannan, Samuel 48, 51, 62, 115
Broderick, David C. 13, 33, 35, 37, 45, 53, 62, 66, 68, 72, 73, 75, 82, 100, 115
Broderick-Terry 1859 duel 74
Brown, John 58, 78
Buchanan, James 19, 70, 73, 82, 86
Burnett, Peter 20, 24, 49, 59

C

Calhoun, John C. 42
Californian, The 49
California Star 19, 49, 115
California Theatre 69, 110
Californios 21, 25, 31, 61
Chivs (Chivalry Southerners) 6, 56, 68, 73, 81
Clay, Henry 42, 86
Colton Hall 20, 22
Compromise of 1850 42, 44

Index

Constitutional Convention of 1849 18, 21, 24, 49
customhouse 18, 20, 45, 55, 92

D

Daily Alta California 10, 13, 51, 56, 61, 94, 115
Daily Dramatic Chronicle 10, 35, 105, 118
Davis, Jefferson 42, 62, 91, 92, 112
Democratic Party 47, 64, 68, 70, 76, 78, 83, 101
de Young, Charles 9
de Young, Gustavus 9, 131
de Young, Michael 127, 131
Douglas, Stephen A. 43, 83
duels 6, 74, 76, 90, 129

E

election
  of 1852 47
  of 1856 70
  of 1860 82
  of 1864 101
Ellis, Alfred J. 21
Evans, George Henry 38

F

Fillmore, Millard 43, 47, 89
fires 32, 35, 53, 102, 105
Folsom, Joseph 52, 55, 56, 61, 65
Foote, Henry 43, 62, 68
Fort Mason 91, 99
Fort Point 88, 92, 105
Fort Sumter 86, 88, 92
Free-Soil Party 39, 47, 77

Frémont, Jessie Benton 22, 25, 52, 71, 80, 84, 87, 99, 109
Frémont, John C. 22, 25, 28, 43, 52, 70, 80, 84, 87, 89, 95, 99, 109

G

Geary, John W. 72, 86, 95
Gilbert, Edward 21, 25, 51
Golden Gate 12, 16, 28, 34, 43, 60, 88
Grant, Ulysses S. 55, 95, 105, 113, 115
Gwin, William M. 20, 24, 25, 41, 43, 44, 53, 62, 68, 72, 74, 77, 83, 92, 94, 112

H

Halleck, Henry W. 24, 51, 55, 65, 106, 109
Halleck, Peachy and Billings 65, 84, 95, 110
Harpers Ferry 58, 59, 78
Haskell, Leonidas 76, 87, 99
Hitchcock, Charles 55, 57, 92
Hitchcock (Coit), Lillie 55, 57, 95, 116
Hounds 61

J

Jenny Lind Theatre 12
J.M. Chapman 100
Johnson, J. Neely 64, 68, 74
Johnston, Albert Sidney 92, 95

140

INDEX

K

Keene, Laura 16, 103, 110, 112
King of William, James 65
King, Thomas Butler 20, 24, 25, 41, 43, 44, 113
King, Thomas Starr 80, 81, 84, 85, 86, 96, 99, 109
Knights of the Golden Circle (KGC) 92
Know-Nothing Party 62, 64, 68
Kohler, Frederick 37, 54, 56

L

Larkin, Thomas O. 19, 20, 51
Lee, Archy 59, 60
Lincoln, Abraham 10, 33, 37, 43, 67, 70, 71, 82, 83, 84, 85, 86, 92, 94, 97, 98, 99, 100, 101, 102, 103, 104, 105, 106, 108, 109, 113, 116, 118
Long Wharf (Commercial Street) 13, 31
Los Angeles 22, 73, 92, 95, 109

M

Maguire's Opera House 15, 35, 80
Maguire, Tom 12, 13, 34, 35, 68, 97, 112
Mason, Richard 19, 52, 99
McAllister, (Matthew) Hall 62
Metropolitan Theatre 16
Mexican Alta California 5, 18, 19, 23, 48
Mexican-American War 22, 40, 41, 52, 56, 82, 95
mint 38, 69, 92, 97

Monterey 18, 20, 21, 46, 49, 51, 52, 53
Montgomery Block 65, 110
Montgomery, John 18

N

New York 17, 33, 34, 37, 38, 53, 56, 61, 68, 100, 102, 103, 104, 109, 110, 111, 112, 116, 118
Northerners 5, 19, 21, 27, 46, 56, 61, 72

P

Pacific Republic 94, 97
People's Party 68
Pierce, Franklin 47, 127
Pleasant, Mary Ellen 30, 57, 58, 59, 60, 116
Polk, James K. 19, 27, 40
Pony Express 84, 92, 94, 96, 118
Portsmouth Square 13, 20, 28, 32, 34, 43, 48, 52, 62, 72, 77, 105

R

Republican Party 60, 68, 70, 71, 79, 82, 83, 84, 98
Riley, Bennet 19, 22, 41
Roberts, Sam 61, 62
Robinson, David "Yankee" 34, 57, 112

S

Sacramento 13, 49, 52, 59, 64, 72, 74, 92

INDEX

San José 25
Scott, William 85
Secessionists 84, 92, 95, 101, 105
Shakespeare, William 32, 97, 102, 104, 110, 116, 118
Sherman, William Tecumseh 16, 22, 24, 25, 51, 52, 68, 70, 84, 95, 116
slavery 5, 6, 19, 23, 25, 38, 40, 41, 42, 46, 49, 53, 59, 64, 70, 72, 73, 78, 80, 83, 100
Southerners 5, 19, 27, 41, 42, 45, 46, 47, 48, 56, 71, 72, 73, 78, 81, 94, 95, 116
Stevenson, Jonathan 37, 56
Stevenson's Regiment 56, 61
Sydney Ducks 62

T

Taylor, Zachary 20, 40, 41, 43, 52
telegraph 9, 35, 86, 96, 106, 118
Telegraph Hill 12, 28, 35, 57, 94, 112, 118
Terry, David 59, 66, 74, 75, 76, 96, 115

U

Union Square 86

V

Vigilance Committee
 of 1851 62, 66
 of 1856 67, 68

W

Webster, Daniel 42, 86
Weller, John 47, 55, 72, 73, 74
West Point 52, 55, 94
Whig Party 20, 40, 41, 47, 64, 70
Wilmot Proviso 40, 41, 42

Y

Yerba Buena 18, 28, 48, 52
 Cove 28, 31, 37, 55

About the Author

Monika Trobits is a San Francisco resident of more than thirty years. She has been studying San Francisco's history and politics since the mid-1980s. Her interest in the Civil War and the theater began during her formative years in New York City. A performance of the opera *Appomattox* at the San Francisco Opera House in 2007, followed by a two-day seminar at Stanford University in 2009 entitled "Lincoln and the West," reawakened Monika's interest in the antebellum/Civil War eras. She began to explore the role that California and specifically San Francisco had played in years leading up to and during the war. That endeavor turned into a multi-year project and led to this book. In addition to her work in the corporate world, Monika has been a docent/tour guide for various historically based organizations and local tour operators for more than twenty years. These include the California Historical Society, the San Francisco Museum and Historical Society, San Francisco Urban Adventures and San Francisco Sightseeing. For many years, she led tours through the History Gallery of the Oakland Museum of California and at San Francisco's majestic city hall. Her article "Dashiell Hammett's San Francisco in the 1920s" was published in the San Francisco–based *Argonaut*, a historic journal. Monika earned a bachelor's

About the Author

degree in political science/history from San Francisco State University. She lives at Lake Merced, just down the road from the site of the 1859 Broderick-Terry duel. In 2011, Monika established her own walking tour company: San Francisco Journeys. She has developed a walking tour in conjunction with this book. Information may be found on www.sanfranciscojourneys.com.